KINGDOM DYNAMICS

FOR DOMINATING IN CHRIST

ALLEN FORBES

Kingdom Dynamics For Dominating In Christ
Copyright © 2018 by Allen Forbes
ISBN-10: 0-9977123-2-5
ISBN-13: **978-0-9977123-2-2**

Printed in the United States of America. All rights reserved under international copyright law. Contents and/or cover may not be reproduced in whole or part without the express written consent of the publisher.

Published by Alloy Consulting Group LLC
P.O. Box 305
Germantown, MD 20875

Library of Congress Control Number: 2018905544

Scripture quotations marked KJV are taken from the King James Version of the bible

Scripture quotations marked NKJV are taken from the New King James Version®. Copyright © 1982 by Thomas Nelson. Used by permission. All rights reserved.

Scripture quotations marked GW are taken from GOD'S WORD®, © 1995 God's Word to the Nations. Used by permission of Baker Publishing Group.

Cover design by Tracy Jackson
MediaCyctems

Dedicated

In loving memory of

Rosa Lee Forbes

June 18, 1932 - December 5, 2007

May you dominate in life through Christ!

Table of Contents

Acknowledgements 1
Foreword 3
INTRODUCTION 5

Part 1 Kingdom Functionality 13
Chapter 1 Kingdom Occupation 15
Chapter 2 Kingdom Functioning 27
Chapter 3 A Heart For The Kingdom 37

Part 2 Exposing the Kingdom of Darkness 55
Chapter 4 The Enemy's Playbook 57

Part 3 Kingdom Domination 77
Chapter 5 Kingdom Thinking 79
Chapter 6 Kingdom Image 89
Chapter 7 Seeing It 109

Reference 127
About the Author 129
Resources 131

Acknowledgements

I'd like to say thank you:
To the many friends, professional editors and readers of my manuscript who proofed, edited and provided thoughtful, wise and fearless feedback of this Kingdom assignment. I'm truly blessed and honored that I know you! Specifically, to –

Connie Howard and Bobbette Gordon for your editing gifts.

Jean Williams, Yetty Logan, TK Falayi and Reggie Coleman for your valuable kingdom feedback on my manuscript.

Tracy Jackson for your cover design.

To my lovely wife Lloyda Forbes for your writing and editorial contributions and for always believing in me.

Pastor Dwayne Brewington (Pastor "Brew") for being a man of God with a Word from God and for inspiring me to be all that God has called me to be.

Finally, to all who will enjoy this book. This book is from God's heart to mine, and now to you.

Thank you all!

Foreword

As a Pastor, I often find the necessity of teaching and preaching things over and over again. People don't get things because they "heard" it once, twice, or even ten times! Subjects like love, faith, prosperity and commitment must be repeated to keep them "fresh" in the hearts and minds of believers. Well, another subject that needs to be refreshed often is who we are in Christ and the authority that he has given us. In this book "Kingdom Dynamics For Dominating In Christ" Minister Allen Forbes has captured that truth in a simple but profound way! He shows us how to identify where we are, the strategies of the enemy, and ultimately how to manifest our God given authority and DOMINATE! This book is a reference tool that you can read repeatedly to remind you of who you are and what you have and can do in Christ! Now, go ahead and get started reading and begin to reign and rule in life! DOMINATE!

Romans 5:17 KJV
For if by one man's offence death reigned by one; much more they which receive abundance of grace and of the gift of righteousness <u>shall reign in life by one</u>, Jesus Christ.

Pastor Dwayne Brewington

Victory Christian Church International

www.vcci.org

INTRODUCTION
Give Him a Key

When I finally turned 12, my mother and father had decided after a long deliberation to finally give me a key to the house. I was the youngest and my dad always thought that one of the kids was going to lose the key and he would have to change all of the locks. They had come to an agreement that I was going to have a key. All was well until I started hanging out with the 'bad kids' in middle school. I remember one day a group of us played hooky from school. Somehow we ended up at my house hanging out and watching TV. My mother and father were both at work so we had the entire house to ourselves. We arrived around 11 AM and my mother was not due home until after 2 PM. After hanging out and having a few snacks, around 1:15 or so I decided to go out to the front yard to get some air. I remember looking up the street and seeing my mother walking down toward the house. I was horrified! She was early! In a fit of panic I ran into the house and screamed, "My mother is coming"! Everyone quickly jumped up and I hurried them toward the back of the house into the backyard. My mother came in and I met her at the door to let her know that I was home early because I did not feel well— yes, I lied. She came inside, and for some reason she did not take her seat in front of the TV to watch her favorite soap opera. Instead, she moved around the house and ended up in the kitchen to get something to eat. As God would have it, for some reason the Holy Spirit led her to the backyard where my friends were hiding. She was shocked to find my friends hiding in the corner huddling together. She immediately grabbed a broom and began swinging it at them chasing them out of the yard as she hollered, "Get out of my house"! After she chased them out of the yard through the house, she turned to me and reprimanded me for having people in the house when no one else was home. I felt terrible because after mom settled down she expressed her disappointment in me for not being responsible. I had betrayed her trust. Eventually she forgave me, but I learned two important lessons:

1) With authority comes responsibility.
2) Mom knew that she had authority and used that authority to chase out the unwanted guests in her home.

How many times do we allow things to just keep going on and not take authority over them? **What we allow will continue.** Jesus did not allow what was not God's will, to continue. However, others (religious leaders) who were unsure of their authority went about their days with business-as-usual. The following is an example of Jesus using His authority to discontinue an unwanted event...

Mark 1:21-27 KJV

²¹ And they went into Capernaum; and straightway on the sabbath day he entered into the synagogue, and taught. ²² And they were astonished at his doctrine: for he taught them as one that had authority, and not as the scribes. ²³ And there was in their synagogue a man with an unclean spirit; and he cried out, ²⁴ Saying, Let us alone; what have we to do with thee, thou Jesus of Nazareth? art thou come to destroy us? I know thee who thou art, the Holy One of God. ²⁵ And Jesus rebuked him, saying, Hold thy peace, and come out of him.²⁶ And when the unclean spirit had torn him, and cried with a loud voice, he came out of him. ²⁷ And they were all amazed, insomuch that they questioned among themselves, saying, What thing is this? what new doctrine is this? for with authority commandeth he even the unclean spirits, and they do obey him.

Jesus and His disciples entered into Capernaum which means "village of comfort". This was a flourishing city on the west side of the Lake of Gennesaret near where the Jordan River flows into the lake. On the Sabbath day Jesus entered into the synagogue and began to teach. There was a clear difference between how Jesus taught and how the scribes taught. The difference was that He clearly had authority. **Real authority cannot be faked**.

To have **genuine authority** you have to be authorized. The word *authorized* means to *give authority or power to*. The top of the authority chain always goes back to the author or owner. The word *author* means the *maker of anything, creator* or *originator*. Jesus knew the Author (God) because He was one with God and had been authorized with His authority to carry out His will. There is also such a thing as **self-authorizing**. As you may have guessed, this is authority that is not properly delegated. This is what the people in Capernaum were used to seeing in the synagogue. There is a definite difference between the two. One type has real power and the other is just talk. Real authority is knowing that you have been authorized and having a deep conviction of this truth. Authority moves things, people, and resources. It makes changes, stops activities and takes control. You either have it or not.

Here in Capernaum we have an unclean spirit encapsulated in a man who is in a synagogue within a flourishing city in a comfortable place. [Isn't it interesting that the devil goes to church?!] The devil is so happy in this flourishing economy and so comfortable in that place, that he becomes indignant with Jesus. He begins to cry out to Jesus saying, "Let us alone, what do you want with us? Are you here to destroy us, we know who you are, you are the Holy One of God" (my interpretation).

Jesus rebukes the unclean spirit saying, "Hold thy peace, and come out of him". Note: *Jesus rebuked by saying*, He used His authority by <u>saying</u>. While it is true that you exercise your authority by saying, Jesus did not speak to get His authority to move; He actually spoke because <u>He had</u> authority, and then His authority moved. He said, "Hold thy peace". This phrase means to "remain silent". Once Jesus spoke this, the demon could no longer talk because He took away his authority to speak. This is not like when we see someone arrested and the cop puts on the handcuffs and says, "You have the right to remain silent". Jesus was not saying you have the right to remain silent, He was saying "remain silent, speak no more (shut up)". This meant that even if the devil wanted to speak, he could not. His voice was taken away by the author of all sound!

There are some settings in your life that have been speaking loud and proud for a long time and it's time to silence and take authority over them. <u>Jesus used His authority to stop the demonic activity in this man and to cast out the unclean spirit</u>. It is my prayer that you will begin to use your God-given authority to make changes, stop unwanted activity, and take control over your life. God wants you to walk in these Kingdom keys for dominating in your life through Christ. As you read this book, may your eyes be opened to see God's good, perfect and acceptable will for your life, and may you dominate in life through Christ. *This is your time!*

Part 1

Kingdom Functionality

Chapter 1

Kingdom Occupation

Moving Forward

I used to work at the Pentagon and it is estimated that anywhere from 22,000 to 23,000 people enter the building every day. That's a huge office building! A plane crashed into it in 2001 and not even one-fifth of the building was destroyed. That's how big the building is. When you enter into the Pentagon and walk down the corridor – depending on where you come in – you will make it to the main ring, which is called the 'A Ring'. When you get to the 'A Ring, there is a directory telling you how to get around the Pentagon. Even if you have a room number that you are trying to get to, and you can see it on the map, it won't do you any good unless you see that little square symbol that says "**You are here**". Many people want to do great things but they are unsure of how to get there. Before you get started, the first thing you will have to do is to identify where you are and where you want to go in life.

In order to get to Point B, you've got to establish where Point A is. This works in every area of your life: finances, marriage, business, career, etc. First find where you would like to go. Then identify where you are currently. You could wander and make it to the right place by chance, or you can get to where you want to go on purpose. It will be a lot shorter and easier to get there *on purpose*. Remember the children of Israel wandered 40 years in the wilderness before they entered the Promise Land. **Identifying where you are allows you to measure the progress that you are making toward your destination**. This is why you must be truthful with yourself when self-evaluating.

I remember personally going through a rough season in my life. It was difficult because I did not have any direction. I did not know where I wanted to go, nor did I know where I was (Point A). I only knew that somehow I was not where I was supposed to be. This caused me to be frustrated and unproductive. The funny thing is, looking at me you could not tell all that I was dealing with. I had a good marriage, nice car and a good job. However, I was unfulfilled because I had all these dreams that God had put inside of me... all these things that I would think about doing. Then my mind would shut down and say, "There is no way you could do that! It is too big!" So I did nothing. I continued to be frustrated and didn't make any progress. You may be in the same situation. You have these dreams and these ideas that God has given you, and you've had them for a long time and you have just kind of given up on them. I am submitting to you that you don't have to. The fact that you are still thinking about them means that there is life in them, and life in you!

Napoleon Hill – a writer and a very successful businessman from the 1900's wrote a book called [a] "The Principles of Self Mastery". One of the principles he identified in the book is "Your Definite Chief Aim". This principle states the importance of knowing where you are aspiring to go. Where does God want you to go? You must establish a chief aim in life. There are major areas in your life that have to be targeted in order to be reached. Write down a 1, 3, 5, and 10-year aim. Then work backwards, in order to figure out how you're going to get there.

Plan and research

Once you establish Point A and Point B, you have to develop a plan to get there. How do you move forward? If there are certain areas of your life that seem like they are getting away from you, that you have no control over, you may need to sit down and figure out a plan for dealing with those areas and attaining your 'definite chief aim.'

> **Luke 14:28-31** [NKJV]
> [28] *For which of you, intending to build a tower, does not sit down first and count the cost, whether he has enough to finish it—* [29] *lest, after he has laid the foundation, and is not able to finish, all who see it begin to mock him,* [30] *saying, 'This man began to build and was not able to finish'?* [31] *Or what king, going to make*

war against another king, does not sit down first and consider whether he is able with ten thousand to meet him who comes against him with twenty thousand?

Notice this pivotal point Jesus is making; He is saying you have to develop a plan. He is saying you don't build or go to war without having a plan. **A plan is a necessity for moving forward in life.** Do not forget that you have an enemy and his job is to try to get you off of God's plan for your life. He will try to distract you from being all that God has called you to be. Many times what will happen is, through the decisions we make, we create an entrance for the devil to come in and mess around in our stuff (Gen 3:1-19). Then, we become reactionary: "Oh, this just happened." "There's a fire here! Let me get some water on this one!" Then while that fire is blazing, something else starts sparking in another area, and you say, "Oh, let me do something with this." It becomes so easy to become distracted. Remember that it is a good *defense* strategy that helps to win games. However, if you never score you will lose the game. It is time to launch an *offensive plan* that causes you to reach your expected end. **It is time for an offensive plan!** Do not stay in a reactionary mode to what happens in life. Instead plan, so that you can just respond because you already have a plan in place. Do not be scared to do what God has told you to do. *Research and plan!*

[a] Napoleon Hill had an instance where he needed $25,000. He wanted to start a school to help people in sales and in advertising. [This is in 1916, so you can imagine how much money that would be by today's standards.] So he took six weeks to think and plan. He thought about what he wanted and needed. He needed the money and the course. He didn't have any of the money, but he did have the course that he wanted to teach. After the six weeks of planning, thinking, and trying to figure out how he was going to get $25,000, he had an **idea**. He went to a school that was already in operation, and gave this sales pitch to the owner of the school: Mr. Hill said, *"I'd like to teach this course I have developed at your school and this will benefit you because the times are hard and people are picking other colleges besides yours. It will help draw students back to your school and you can charge them tuition. I just want to be able to run the department. You spend your money on advertising for it. When that tuition comes in from my course, use it to pay the expense of advertising. Plus you'll be drawing other people to other parts of your school".* The owner listened intently and Mr. Hill continued. *"Here is what I would like out of this deal. When the advertising bill has been paid, I just want to be able to run the school on my own."* The owner of the school said, "Fine." Less than a

year later the advertising costs had all been paid by tuition and Napoleon Hill had the school, debt free.

Mr. Hill thought that he needed to come up with $25,000 but what he really needed was *an idea*. There are always other ways to get finances. It does not always have to come from a bank. You have *ideas*. You have *creativity*. You have dreams and purpose that God has breathed into you and *you can do it*. Do not let anyone tell you that you can't. Mr. Hill took six weeks of planning to come up with a win/win solution to his dilemma. The better thought-out the plan, the easier it will be to implement it. The less thought-out the plan the more execution is needed, because you will hit hurdles that you did not think about. Make sure that you build recovery strategies into your plans in case things don't work out as originally planned.

> **Luke 16:1-8** NKJV
>
> *He also said to His disciples: "There was a certain rich man who had a steward, and an accusation was brought to him that this man was wasting his goods. 2 So he called him and said to him, 'What is this I hear about you? Give an account of your stewardship, for you can no longer be steward. 3 "Then the steward said within himself, 'What shall I do? For my master is taking the stewardship away from me. I cannot dig; I am ashamed to beg. 4 I have resolved what to do, that when*

> *I am put out of the stewardship, they may receive me into their houses.'* ⁵*"So he called every one of his master's debtors to him, and said to the first, 'How much do you owe my master?'* ⁶*And he said, 'A hundred measures of oil.' So he said to him, 'Take your bill, and sit down quickly and write fifty.'* ⁷*Then he said to another, 'And how much do you owe?' So he said, 'A hundred measures of wheat.' And he said to him, 'Take your bill, and write eighty.'* ⁸*So the master commended the unjust steward because he had dealt shrewdly. For the sons of this world are more shrewd in their generation than the sons of light.*

I would like to bring this story up-to-date in today's time and in today's vernacular. The steward is wasting his boss's goods. He's not doing what he's supposed to do. So his boss says, "Look, you have done a terrible job managing my affairs and you have been wasting my goods. You're fired!" Watch what the steward does next. The steward says within himself "What shall I do?" He considered the situation and resolved what to do. He did not worry…not at all. In thinking <u>what should I do</u>, the steward approached this situation from a standpoint of planning his next move. He was not wondering, "Oh, my goodness, what am I going to do?"

³ *"Then the steward said within himself, 'What shall I do? For*

my master is taking the stewardship away from me. I cannot dig; I am ashamed to beg. [4] I have resolved what to do...

We would put it this way; I know what I'm going to do. *[4]...that when I am put out of the stewardship, they may receive me into their houses.' [5] "So he called every one of his master's debtors to him, and said to the first, 'How much do you owe my master?' [6] And he said, 'A hundred measures of oil.' So he said to him, 'Take your bill, and sit down quickly and write fifty.' [7] Then he said to another, 'And how much do you owe?' So he said, 'A hundred measures of wheat.' And he said to him, 'Take your bill, and write eighty.'*

You see what he is doing? He is doing what I call a master hustle! He is thinking, *I need to make new friends because I am going to be out with my existing boss, so let me set up some other relationships for later.*

Verse 8 of this passage of scripture is the part that always perplexed me. The master **commended** the unjust steward because he had dealt **shrewdly**. I would always wonder why?

[8] ...because he had dealt shrewdly. For the sons of this world are more shrewd in their generation than the sons of light.

Now, I understand the point that Jesus was making in this

parable. He was saying that the children of the world are *wiser* in the ways that the world works ... and in working the world's system to their advantage. However, the children of light are not as wise (as it relates to) working the methods that God has set up for them to work. He's talking *methods*. The Kingdom of God is a *method* (system) that the children of Light need to master. However, before it can be mastered, you – as a child of Light, must understand how you were created to function in the Kingdom.

Children of the World

I read about a millionaire who said that when he lost all his money he realized that he stopped doing some things that he used to do which made him successful. He used to spend three hours a day in quiet time, meditating (the children of this world are wiser than the children of Light). He had stopped the practice of spending quiet time flipping through books and going through magazines that gave him ideas for new trends, and he subsequently lost his entire fortune. So, he began to do those things all over again, consistently. Now he's recovered the fortune that was lost, and he is now a billionaire.

This concept and methodology works for the man that is born-again and the man that is not. That is why there are people who are successful in the world (by the world's standards). However, you also have the same system/methodology and opportunity set up *within* you! You have God on your side (the Big Plus). You just have to do it. When you take what God has said about you (His Word) and meditate on the word, He will give you ideas that will benefit not just yourself but all those around you.

Note: Success isn't always just about money. No – you need success to have a good marriage, a healthy body and everything else that concerns your life. God's success includes money and every other area of your life. What good would it do you if you gained riches and fame and your family went to hell? **God's plan for your success is all-inclusive**. No other plan will cover you like God's plan for your success. Let's look at how you were created to function.

Chapter 2

Kingdom Functioning

Understanding How You Are Created To Function

Kingdom Function: The method (system) in which you were created to operate.

> **Genesis 2:7** *NKJV*
> *⁷ And the LORD God formed man of the dust of the ground, and breathed into his nostrils the breath of life; and man became a living being.*

God is working in the Garden, and He's forming man out of dust (ground). The Bible says, He breathes into him the breath of life and man became a living soul (being). Here we have God blowing His Spirit into mankind to give them *His* life. As God blew into each of us with His inspired breath, whatever He was thinking about at the time *is our unique purpose.* Just like His word cannot return to Him void, neither can His breath. **This is why we <u>must</u> fulfill His purpose for our lives.** Our purpose is not external where just anyone can get to it. It is deposited within where it cannot be disturbed or destroyed. It is *discovered* by the beholder.

> **Genesis 2:15** *KJV*
> *And the LORD God took the man, and put him into the garden of Eden to dress it and to keep it.*

The word <u>dress</u> means to till. <u>Till</u> means to bring forth. He put man into the garden to cause the garden to come forth. Keep means to guard and to protect. Man has two jobs; one is to Till – or to bring forth, and the other is to Keep – to guard. These are the two things that man was commissioned to do. God was sharing with man (male and female) that they were made out of the dust (ground), so they could see how the ground functions and how they also function internally. In other words, your heart is like the ground. When a seed is planted in the ground it will bring forth what was planted. So God is trying to not only have them (mankind) see this concept physically, but He also wants them to understand the spiritual concept as well, "**You are actually ground, and there is a garden within**". The ground will bring forth what is planted in it. Plant wisely and keeping this in mind, let's look at the parable of the sower.

> ***Matthew 13:1-9*** *KJV*
>
> *The same day went Jesus out of the house, and sat by the sea side. ² And great multitudes were gathered together unto him, so that he went into a ship, and sat; and the whole multitude stood on the shore. ³ And he spake many things unto them in parables, saying, Behold, a sower went forth to sow; ⁴ And when he sowed, some seeds fell by the way side, and the fowls came and devoured them up: ⁵ Some fell upon stony places, where they had not much earth: and forthwith they sprung up, because they had no deepness of*

> earth: ⁶ *And when the sun was up, they were scorched; and because they had no root, they withered away.* ⁷ *And some fell among thorns; and the thorns sprung up, and choked them:* ⁸ *But other fell into good ground, and brought forth fruit, some an hundredfold, some sixtyfold, some thirtyfold* ⁹ *Who hath ears to hear, let him hear.*

In the parable of the sower, the Sower sows seed in 4 places: 1) on the wayside, 2) upon rocky ground, 3) on thorns (tares), and 4) some on good ground. Then Jesus explains the parable...

> **Matthew 13:19-23** KJV
> ¹⁹ *When any one heareth the* **word of the kingdom**, *and understandeth it not, then cometh the wicked one, and catcheth away that which was sown in his heart. This is he which received seed by the way side.* ²⁰ *But he that received the seed into stony places, the same is he that heareth the word, and anon with joy receiveth it;* ²¹ *Yet hath he not root in himself, but dureth for a while: for when tribulation or persecution ariseth because of the word, by and by he is offended.* ²² *He also that received seed among the thorns is he that heareth the word; and the care of this world, and the deceitfulness of riches, choke the word, and he becometh unfruitful.* ²³ *But he that received seed into the good ground is he that heareth the word, and understandeth it; which also*

> *beareth fruit, and bringeth forth, some an hundredfold, some* sixty, some thirty.

In Matthew 13, Jesus is basically saying that He is sowing the word, which is equated to seed. Some seeds are falling on the wayside; some folk aren't hearing it at all, and immediately the devil comes in and steals the word right out of their heart. Then He also says that some seeds are sown on stony ground. For a short while something pops up but then, because of tribulation for the word's sake, it shrivels up. He goes on to say that other words (seeds) are sown amongst the tares. The tares are going to grow up and choke it. The tares are actually cares of the world and the deceitfulness of riches. [Note: Not riches, but the deceitfulness of it.] Finally, He says that there is a fourth ground and that is good ground. It's going to produce some thirty, some sixty, and some hundredfold return (of the seed that's sown into it)".

Jesus makes an analogy between the heart of man and the ground that a farmer uses for his seed. Everything God does He does with a purpose. In Genesis 2, He put man in the garden and He put the garden into man. Jesus reveals this to us in this parable. Once the word is sown it is up to the individual to manage their garden (heart), to protect, keep, and bring forth fruit. That is how you produce as a Christian. He wants us to take this whole concept/ideology of the garden to heart and liken it to the Kingdom of God. **Where is the Kingdom of God? The Kingdom of God is <u>within</u> you** (Luke 17:21).

If I took a piece of metal, bent it into a rim for my car and put a tire on it, this would not change the fact that the rim is still a piece of metal. So the rim is still under the <u>same laws</u> that apply to and affect metal. Likewise, you are created to function a certain way. Physically, you were made from the ground, and your heart – not your physical heart, but the spiritual side of you, is like ground. It's the place where everything grows/flows from… where your issues of life flow out of. Your heart is just like ground, where seeds grow and it produces a harvest off of that seed. God put man into the garden to work the sowing and tending process and cause the garden to come forth, so man could know and see how he is created to function. Therefore, while man was working on the external garden, God's purpose was to get man to understand that there was a garden on the *inside of them (mankind – male and female)*. No other creature on this planet has that capacity. That's what gives you authority. You can *choose* what seeds you decide to plant inside your heart. No animal or anything else on this planet, only the human race that God created in His image and in His likeness has that power. Consider this…if you are in charge of your own garden and you have the seeds in your possession, then what is impossible to you? God is pure genius! While man is tilling (causing to bring forth) and keeping (guarding) the ground, God is showing man how mankind is created to function. What an object lesson!

Jesus used parables so that people could understand the Kingdom of God and how it operates, but they still weren't getting it (see *Mark 4:10-11*). But if you explain this to your children when they're four and five, they're going to latch onto this. Most psychologists believe that by the time a child is eight years old they have their attitudes, mindsets, and their belief system already in place. Many of the behaviors and mindsets we have as adults are developed from our birth to eight years-old (exposure) psyche. If you will pay attention to the habits and the cycles that you follow, you can usually trace them back to your early childhood. In my other book, [b] [Sandbox Personalities](), I get more in depth into the behaviors and why many of us act the way that we do. This is why it is imperative that we teach our children this concept of how God created us to function. If they internalize this while they are young it will affect the rest of their lives in a greater way.

Your heart is your center and it is *the real you*. Out of the abundance of the heart, the mouth speaks (*Luke 6:45*). As a man thinks (where?) in his heart, so is he (*Proverbs 23:7*). Remember, you have two jobs: to till (cause to bring forth) and to keep (to guard and to protect). Adam and Eve let the ball drop when it came to keeping the garden. We can't really fault them because who knows what we probably would have done? When they messed up, God sent Jesus (the Son of His dear Love) to come and restore mankind (us) back to our original position of power, dominion, and authority as it was in the beginning. Jesus used parables to get his disciples and followers to understand that Kingdom power, dominion and authority can be forfeited to the enemy if you do not guard and protect your heart. God sent Jesus to share many illustrations and parables about the Kingdom of God, to get these principles over to man about how mankind was designed to function in the Kingdom.

1) Before mankind can be reinstated to a place of victory, dominion, control and authority, we have to understand how (and why) we were created to function.

2) There is a garden within mankind and it is their responsibility to till the ground, guard it, and bring forth the garden.

3) The heart is ground. Plant seeds wisely as the ground will bring forth what has been planted.

Chapter 3

A Heart For The Kingdom

The Power Center

Have you ever wondered why things and situations responded whenever Jesus spoke to them? For example, how a fig tree would dry up from His words (Mark 11:20-21)? How a man who was paralyzed would respond to Jesus' words by getting up and carrying the bed that he was just laying on (Luke 5:24-25)? Or, how He could call a young girl who was laying dead on her bed, back to life (Mark 5:41-42)? Of course, we know that He is Jesus (the Son of God) and the Spirit was given to Him without measure (John 3:34). However, He would get upset when His disciples (those He was teaching about the Kingdom of God) could not perform at the level He wanted them to (Mark 4:40). I believe a big key is what you are about to discover in the following passages...

> **Luke 4:1-14** NKJV
>
> *Then Jesus, being filled with the Holy Spirit, returned from the Jordan and was led by the Spirit into the wilderness, ² being tempted for forty days by the devil. And in those days He ate nothing, and afterward, when they had ended, He was hungry. ³ And the devil said to Him, "If You are the Son of God, command this stone to become bread." ⁴ But Jesus answered him, saying, "It is written, 'Man shall not live by bread alone, but by every word of God.'" ⁵ Then the devil, taking Him up on a high mountain, showed Him all the kingdoms of the world in a moment of time. ⁶ And the devil said to Him, "All this*

authority I will give You, and their glory; for this has been delivered to me, and I give it to whomever I wish. ⁷ Therefore, if You will worship before me, all will be Yours." ⁸ And Jesus answered and said to him, "Get behind Me, Satan! For it is written, 'You shall worship the Lord your God, and Him only you shall serve.' " ⁹ Then he brought Him to Jerusalem, set Him on the pinnacle of the temple, and said to Him, "If You are the Son of God, throw Yourself down from here. ¹⁰ For it is written: 'He shall give His angels charge over you, To keep you,'¹¹ and, 'In their hands they shall bear you up, Lest you dash your foot against a stone.'" ¹² And Jesus answered and said to him, "It has been said, 'You shall not tempt the Lord your God.' " ¹³ Now when the devil had ended every temptation, he departed from Him until an opportune time.¹⁴ Then Jesus returned in the power of the Spirit to Galilee, and news of Him went out through all the surrounding region.

In Luke 4:1-14 we see that the devil tried to come against Him three different times. Jesus used the Word of God as a defense against the thoughts and words of the devil. He used the Word <u>defensively</u> in those three encounters. The heart of Jesus (His 'ground') was pure. He didn't have a bunch of junk (doubt, fear, hatred and death) in there. Let's look at what happens a little later in the same chapter, after His bout with the devil.

LUKE 4:31-36 NKJV

31 Then He went down to Capernaum, a city of Galilee, and was teaching them on the Sabbaths. 32 And they were astonished at His teaching, for His word was with authority. 33 Now in the synagogue there was a man who had a spirit of an unclean demon. And he cried out with a loud voice, 34 saying, "Let us alone! What have we to do with You, Jesus of Nazareth? Did You come to destroy us? I know who You are—the Holy One of God!" 35 But Jesus rebuked him, saying, "Be quiet, and come out of him!" And when the demon had thrown him in their midst, it came out of him and did not hurt him. 36 Then they were all amazed and spoke among themselves, saying, "What a word this is! For with authority and power He commands the unclean spirits, and they come out."

Jesus has a pure heart because He guarded and protected it. After Jesus used the word as a defense (by keeping and guarding His heart), He was then able to use His word offensively (which is like tilling the ground). In this instance a demon is saying, 'we know who you are.' But Jesus says, 'silence and come out of him!' Jesus did not listen or submit to the devil's attack earlier. Therefore, He is now able to exercise power, dominion and authority over the demon. Now, *He* commands the devil and his realm! When thoughts come against you from the demonic realm, guard your heart. Keep it pure, and resist those thoughts. You will have a renewed strength to exercise authority over that realm and fight the devil successfully. **Remember, whomever you obey, you are a servant to** (Romans 6:16).

What is your heart?
Think of your heart as a container that stores information (images, thoughts, words). Just like a computer stores these same things on a hard drive—the heart works the same basic way. The information that is stored in the heart comes out under certain situations and circumstances (when the right 'buttons' are pressed). The information that we allow to enter our hearts has a profound effect on our behavior. The information entered into our hearts and stored now determines our emotional and intellectual reactions and responses to various life instances in our future.

> *Matthew 12:34-35 NKJV*
> [34]...*For out of the abundance of the heart the mouth speaks.* [35] *A good man out of the good treasure of his heart brings forth good things, and an evil man out of the evil treasure brings forth evil things.*

Your heart is your subconscious mind; it is the part of you that works automatically. When you operate out of your subconscious, that is *the real you*. Your subconscious is your "below mind". In order for information to register on your subconscious mind, it must first go through your conscious mind. Right now you're reading this with your conscious mind. Studies show that two weeks from today you will only remember a small percentage of what you're reading right now. When you reread or listen to the same information at least seven times, your subconscious gets it and 80% or higher of the information is retained. This allows you to keep or register the information that you have heard. You are created to act on the repetitious information that is received into your mind/heart. That is why Jesus explained to us that *out of the abundance of the heart does the mouth speak*. Not only do we speak out of the abundance of the heart but we also act out of the abundance of our hearts. The heart is also the muscle that you believe with. Your belief system is formed by what is in your heart. So, not only does it determine what you believe…more importantly, it affects what you don't believe. God is genius, once again!

Because Jesus likened the heart of man to soil (Matt 13:19-23), it is important to understand what soil is, what it does and where it comes from. Soil comes from a rock or the earth. If water on top of a rock freezes, it causes the rock to break and to crumble. In some instances water runs against the rock (like on a riverbed), and causes the rock to break down over a period of time. Erosion also occurs when the rock (earth) wears away, by wind, ice, or most commonly, water. These are some of the ways by which we end up with soil. Now, the soil has to be the right condition for certain seeds to take hold and grow well. The condition of the rock or the earth determines the condition of the soil that results. Every type of soil is not recommended for every type of seed. You have to know what your soil/ground is made up of before you plant the seed...if you want a good harvest. **It is the condition of the soil (heart) that causes things to grow or not grow.**

The 5 Laws of the Heart

1) c Law of Sympathetic Resonance
There is a law in physics called Sympathetic Resonance. Let me explain: If I had two acoustic pianos on opposite sides of a room, and I hit a C note on one, the law goes into effect and causes the C note on the other piano to vibrate or resonate without anyone touching it. This is what I call having harmony, or agreement. The law of Sympathetic Resonance is also evident when sound energy is converted to mechanical energy. Your mouth has a direct correlation to your heart. Your mouth will

sound (speak) whatever is in your heart in abundance (Matthew 12:34). Therefore, consider your mouth as the portal to the Kingdom of God or to the kingdom of darkness. The sounds that you let out of your mouth – when the pressures of life squeeze you, are the sounds that license either kingdom to go into operation (with mechanical action or with material force). Therefore, consider what you are intentionally or accidentally harmonizing or resonating with when you open your mouth to release a sound.

> **Mark 5:24-30 KJV**
>
> *And Jesus went with him; and much people followed him, and thronged him. ²⁵ And a certain woman, which had an issue of blood twelve years, ²⁶ And had suffered many things of many physicians, and had spent all that she had, and was nothing bettered, but rather grew worse, ²⁷ When she had heard of Jesus, came in the press behind, and touched his garment. ²⁸ For **she said**, If I may touch but his clothes, I shall be whole. ²⁹ And straightway the fountain of her blood was dried up; and she felt in her body that she was healed of that plague. ³⁰ And Jesus, immediately knowing in himself that virtue had gone out of him, turned him about in the press, and said, Who touched my clothes?*

This lady (who remains nameless) heard about the

Messiah and the works that He was doing. After hearing about Him, she formulated her thoughts within her heart and said within herself that she just needed to touch The Messiah's clothes and all was going to be well. When her thoughts, words and images became harmonious with the Kingdom of God, she spoke. *This created a miracle within her mouth.* Your words, thoughts and actions have everything to do with the response you subsequently receive or create from the Kingdom of God. She made a sound that resonated with the Kingdom of God. Now she was able to approach the King (Jesus) resonating with Kingdom agreement. Therefore, when she touched His clothes she made contact with the Kingdom of God and all that the Kingdom brings [healing, prosperity, peace, love and joy in the Holy Ghost (Romans14:17)]. **A person who is unified and one with the Kingdom can receive everything that God has to offer.** This is the law of Sympathetic Resonance in action.

2) The Law of Production

> *Matthew 12:35 KJV*
> *35 A good man out of the good treasure of the heart bringeth forth good things: and an evil man out of the evil treasure bringeth forth evil things.*

It would be crazy for a farmer to stand outside on his land and wait for his crop to grow if nothing had been planted in the land. If this were the case, he would have a fruitless season and many wasteful days of waiting for something that was not going to grow. As we discussed earlier, your heart is like the ground (soil) and you get to decide what type of harvest you want by what you choose to plant. The Law of Production and being productive has everything to do with what you do with your time. What you spend your time doing will have either an adverse effect or a favorable outcome in your life. Your heart (ground) will bring forth (produce) whatever is in it in abundance. The heart is neither good nor bad but takes the deposits into the heart and causes them to spring up. Just as the soil does with a natural seed, the heart does with its contents. In order to be fruitful you will need to inject God's word (Kingdom thoughts) into your heart so you can produce with Kingdom capacity.

3) *The Law of Deposit*

> **Matthew 6:21** *KJV*
> [21] *For where your treasure is, there will your heart be also.*

The word *treasure* in Matthew 6:21 means *deposit*. What the scripture is saying is that your heart will be where your deposit is. Your heart is the seat of your appetite, and the treasure or deposit is the information/emotions that you feed on. **What you allow into your heart determines the desires of your heart.**

I remember many years ago my wife discovered this drink called Barleygreen. We would drink it for a health benefit but it had a taste that you would have to experience for yourself. It tasted like grass! Nevertheless, because I wanted the health benefit, I would have one cup of it every morning and frown as I was drinking it. After probably 3 months of this, I would wake up in the morning and I would crave Barleygreen. My body actually had been trained to want this stuff! Looking at this from a natural example of the physical body and food, we can see the correlation between the spiritual side of us and the information we ingest and then begin to crave. The heart is built the same way. The things that we continue to put into it (good or bad) will begin to speak to us. They will cause our spiritual 'appetites' to crave what has been deposited or things related to what has been deposited. Therefore, the things that are repeated, ingested, or seen consistently over time enter the heart and have an effect on our desires.

4) The Law of Environment

If I had a little tree planted in a little pot, the tree probably couldn't grow any bigger than the pot would allow. What would I need to do to make it bigger? Right...I would need a *bigger* pot and *more* soil. Another way of putting it would be that I would need a different environment which would allow the tree to grow to its capacity and also produce. The same is true with you. If you desire to grow more and produce more you will need to change the environment you are in.

People are a big part of our environments. Sometimes relationships can be the biggest and hardest limitations to growth. People and relationships can create a comfortable (and non-productive) living space for themselves and also for you if you are not careful. Therefore, it is advisable to limit your exposure, or even stay away from people who are putting limits on your life by telling you what you can and can't afford or what you can or can't do. I remember years ago when I was at work in my office, surfing the Internet, looking at a Mercedes Benz that had a price tag of $86,000 on it. Someone looking over my shoulder said to me, "Are you going to buy one of those? That is a lot of money!" I mentally and spiritually blocked out those words because as long as I think $86,000 is a lot of money, it's going to be a lot of (too much) money. What I decided was that I just needed an environment change. What I couldn't afford was to have that voice in my head. If you were to do an analysis of some of your friends and those that you hang around, you would probably agree that you might need to do the same. **People give you**

their limitations all of the time and they are unhappy when your thinking outgrows them.

A Word about Friends and your Inner Circle

We let people choose to become our friends and sometimes we are friends for the wrong reasons. Are your friends lifting you up or are you the one who is always doing the lifting in your relationships? If you are the smartest one in the group that you hang with you may think that's good, but it really is not! You can teach others, however it is also very important that you are around people who are teaching you, and taking you to new heights and to new levels. The only real way you will experience change in your circumstances is if you 'transplant' yourself from the environment that you are in to a new one that is conducive to growth and development. This can, and should happen physically and also mentally. This 'transplanting' will allow you to bring forth more fruit and attain the purpose that God has for your life.

I'm not saying you have to totally get rid of your current circle of friends, or your relationships. What I am submitting to you is that it is vitally important for you to have a strong circle of individuals that think bigger than you do and that do bigger things than you do. Even if your friends may be believers that love you and love the Lord, if their vision for life and expectations are limited, they can be some of the biggest hindrances to the dreams and visions that God has deposited within you. I recommend that you search out and be-friend those people who are going to help you move forward. Friendships can be qualified; being intentional with your perception of who is for you or not, and what their purpose is in your life is very helpful for your progress and happiness.

Every successful achiever has inner and outer circles of relationships. You must know who belongs in which circle. Outer circle relationships don't necessarily get the benefit of hearing your dreams and goals because they may not be able to handle them at this time. You just don't let them know, because sometimes you'll say stuff to some people and they'll say, "Oh, you can't do that!" or "Why do you want to do that?" I have to be careful with whom I even share the dreams and visions that God's given me. Sometimes when God shares something that He wants to do in my life, I wonder myself, "Can I really do that?" Just imagine if I mention it to somebody who has <u>less</u> faith than I do. More than likely they will crush my word from the Lord before it grows fully in my heart! I have learned to allow the dream to grow and mature, with a plan for execution. Then I share it.

There has to be a confidence within you first. You have to have, own and know it *first*, cultivate it and then share it with those in your inner circle. The beauty and function of great inner circle relationships is that these individuals can see what you are seeing. They also believe that you can accomplish and achieve those things. The inner circle also helps you to get there. These people will help to provide a positive and affirming environment where your dreams have a chance to flourish. They do not place restrictions and limits on your ideas and dreams. Therefore, cultivate your inner circle to include relationships which incorporate cheerleaders, experts, mentors, motivators and facilitators of your dream.

Another environment change should be the information that you are exposed to. You should make learning your full time job. For some of you it may involve going back to school. For others it may be reading more and educating yourself in your craft, things that interest you, or what you need to know to move to a higher level. It could be learning about the financial markets, real estate investing or artwork, etc. Don't let a day go by when you don't learn something new and of value – especially in this age of information.

5) The Law of Diligence—Guarding the Heart and practicing His Presence

> *Proverbs 4:23* ᴷᴶⱽ
> ²³ *Keep thy heart with all diligence; for out of it are the issues of life.*

You will need to put forth a constant and earnest effort to guard your heart. It is your responsibility to keep the heart (ground) healthy. We understand, if we were preparing a cake and mixing the ingredients, adding dirt to the mix would change the texture and taste of the cake. But somehow we convince ourselves that watching dirt (sex, lies, sickness, lying, stealing and drama) won't affect us. The climate of this world system is so twisted that we don't think shows are interesting unless they have this content.

If you do a television fast and replace that TV time with time with God for three days, you will see how much clearer the voice of God will be. I believe that God is talking to many of us and we can't hear Him because the images that we have allowed into our hearts are now voices making noise from within. **When there are two or**

more voices being heard, confusion is in the midst. So, God's voice is competing with the other voices in your hearts and heads. Many times, Jesus had to get away from the people around Him to make time to hear the Father. What He heard, He obeyed. That is why He could say *I always do what the Father tells/shows me to do* (John 8:28-29). I believe that making this tiny adjustment in our lives will usher in the very presence of God which will then become a catalyst for revival – starting with you! There is a direct correlation between guarding your heart, ushering in the presence of God and hearing God's voice.

It comes down to the question of *how bad do you want it?* Do you want God and His Kingdom enough to give up those other things? I'm not saying you have to quit watching television. I'm not saying you have to quit going to movies or any of that sort of stuff. But do you want Him enough to pursue Him more than the energy and effort you give to those other things? It is really simple. Make your first order of business to spend some quiet/quality time with God. Be led by His Spirit. Pray and then wait to hear from Him. Don't just get up and walk away. I used to pray for an hour and say "okay, I'm done." Sure, God would speak to me during the day and that was good. However, now I take the time to hear God speak to me during my prayer time, rather than just filling my time with doing all of the talking. There's nothing like having that peace. When you first begin doing this, your thoughts are going to be all over the place. Don't despair. It takes practice to slow the mind down. Just keep doing it, over and over again. Let the Word filter every thought that comes in. This way, you can discern God's voice from another's. Capture the thoughts that you need and that line up with God. Capture them. Hold onto them. Keep them. Everything else that doesn't line up with the Word, just let it go. Begin to let God talk to you and direct your paths through His Word and His instructions. **Practice His presence!**

> **Proverbs 8:17** NKJV
> *17 I love those who love me, and those who seek me diligently will find me.*
>
> **Proverbs 12:24** NKJV
> *24 The hand of the diligent will rule, but the lazy man will be put to forced labor.*

Part 2

Exposing the Kingdom of Darkness

Chapter 4

The Enemy's Playbook

The devil has been around for a long time and is quite crafty and subtle. He knows how mankind was created to function and he knows what to throw at them to get them off course. He also has the history of what things the family's generations have succumbed to before us. He and his crew will try every trick in their playbook to make the people of God stumble. He is our enemy.

The awesome thing about Jesus Christ is that He has given us the keys to the Kingdom and has explained to us the enemy's game plan: He doesn't want us to be ignorant of the enemy's devices. We have reviewed the parable of the Sower to see how we are created to function. Jesus also reveals to us the strategy of the enemy in the same parable. Let us take a closer look…

Parable of the Sower

> *Matthew 13:19-23 KJV*
> *[19] When any one heareth the <u>word of the kingdom</u>, and <u>understandeth it not</u>, then cometh the wicked one, and catcheth away that which was sown in his heart. This is he which received seed by the way side. [20] But he that received the seed into stony places, the same is he that heareth the word, and anon with joy receiveth it; [21] Yet hath he not root in himself, but dureth for a while: for when tribulation or persecution ariseth because of the*

> *word, by and by he is offended.* ²² *He also that received seed among the thorns is he that heareth the word; and the care of this world, and the deceitfulness of riches, choke the word, and he becometh unfruitful.* ²³ *But he that received seed into the good ground is he that heareth the word, and understandeth it; which also beareth fruit, and bringeth forth, some an hundredfold, some sixty, some thirty.*

What Jesus is doing in this parable is showing us the strategy of the enemy. The parable of the sower shows us that there are 3 soil (heart) types or elements that are not really conducive to growth. Let's review them now:

Enemy Strategy #1: Doubt
The first time the sower sows the word (seeds) they are sown by the **wayside**. Jesus tells us that the enemy comes in immediately to steal (take) the word away. The way the enemy does this is with doubt. Doubt means *two* or *double*. So, the first way that the enemy comes against us is with doubt or doubleminded-ness. This can look like questioning whether we heard correct, whether what was said was for us, and was it from God? When we doubt who God says that we are or what He says to do, we end up having two minds. James puts it this way, *a double mind is unstable in all of its ways and should not think to receive anything from the Lord* (James 1:6-8 emphasis added).

Looking at the Scripture, we see two instances when the devil came to get the word that was planted in man's heart. One example is with Adam and Eve and the other involves Jesus himself.

> **Genesis 2:16-17** KJV
>
> [16] And the Lord God commanded the man, saying, Of every tree of the garden thou mayest freely eat: [17] But of the tree of the knowledge of good and evil, thou shalt not eat of it: for in the day that thou eatest thereof thou shalt surely die.
>
> **Genesis 3:1** KJV
>
> Now the serpent was more subtil than any beast of the field which the Lord God had made. And he said unto the woman, Yea, hath God said, Ye shall not eat of every tree of the garden?

The devil begins to question what God has said (God's Word) to cast doubt within Eve's heart. Basically he is saying, "God said you can eat from <u>every</u> tree." Remember, when you hear two or more voices, it can cause confusion. Let's look at what Satan tries to do with Jesus right after Jesus was baptized.

> **Matthew 3:16- 4:3** KJV
>
> [16] When He had been baptized, Jesus came up immediately from the water; and behold, the heavens

were opened to Him, and He saw the Spirit of God descending like a dove and alighting upon Him. ⁱ⁷ And suddenly a <u>voice came from heaven</u>, saying, "<u>This is My beloved Son, in whom I am well pleased</u>." Then Jesus was led up by the Spirit into the wilderness to be tempted by the devil. ² And when He had fasted forty days and forty nights, afterward He was hungry. ³ Now when the tempter came to Him, he said, "<u>If You are the Son of God</u>, command that these stones become bread."

Here we have Jesus being baptized and the heavens are opened and God says that *this is My beloved Son*. Then, immediately after, here comes the devil (to Him) to try to take the word out of His heart; trying to cast doubt by saying *If you are the Son of God prove it!* Jesus had to <u>know</u> what God had said about Him. When the enemy tries to cast doubt in your life, you will have to decide that you are going to believe what God says. Take the time to internalize what God has said and decide that you are going to believe Him, regardless. By making a firm decision that you are going to follow God and his Word, you will leave no room for doubt.

Enemy Strategy #2 Temptation

The second strategy of the enemy, according to the parable in Matthew 13, is revealed when the Sower sows the seeds on rocky or stony ground. The stony ground represents tribulation and persecution. In other words, temptation. This is tricky because we can see there is some growth at this stage, but before the fruit can come to full maturity it withers away due to tribulation/persecution and temptation. **Temptation has everything to do with destroying our focus and what we see.** This is the danger of distraction and the importance of laser focus. Let us look back at our examples of Eve and Jesus.

> **Genesis 3:2-5** ^{KJV}
> *² And the woman said unto the serpent, We may eat of the fruit of the trees of the garden: ³ But of the fruit of the tree which is in the midst of the garden, God hath said, Ye shall not eat of it, neither shall ye touch it, lest ye die. ⁴ And the serpent said unto the woman, <u>Ye shall not surely die</u>: ⁵ For God doth know that in the day ye eat thereof, then your <u>eyes shall be opened, and ye shall be as gods,</u> knowing good and evil.*

In this instance, we see the devil tempting Eve by telling her that what God said was not true. He was trying to get her to believe something that God did not say. He tempted her with wanting to be like God. He wanted her to think that she was missing out on something. Note: She was already like God and he was trying to attack her identity and image. **When you don't know or**

understand who you are, according to what God has said about you, you can easily be distracted. Image and identity are everything when it comes to how you resist temptation and how you handle persecution and tribulation. Now, let's look at the other example, with Jesus in the wilderness:

> **Matthew 4: 5-6** ᴷᴶⱽ
> *Then the devil taketh him up into the holy city, and setteth him on a pinnacle of the temple, ⁶ And saith unto him, <u>If thou be the Son of God, cast thyself down</u>: <u>for it is written</u>, He shall give his angels charge concerning thee: and in their hands they shall bear thee up, lest at any time thou dash thy foot against a stone.*

In this example the devil attacks Jesus's *identity* trying to get Jesus to obey him and prove Himself. Our example, of how we should respond, is seen in Jesus' response. Just as He knew who He was, we should also recognize temptation and stand in the knowledge of who (whose) we are. The reason that we know the devil is tempting Jesus here is because of what Jesus says next:

> **Matthew 4:7** ᴷᴶⱽ
> *⁷ Jesus said unto him, It is written again, <u>Thou shalt not tempt</u> the Lord thy God.*

A word about the stony places/Temptations

Temptations can cause us to take detours from where God wants us to go. Temptations happen to the best of us. We should not allow the fact that we have detoured to discourage us. Just get back on track and keep moving forward. For some of us there are some stones (hard places) that we must surrender to God for His removal. Good things will not last in a stony or hard place, no matter how much seed we put there. Things will wither, simply because the ground is stony (prone to persecution or temptation of some kind).

Having a real relationship with the King (God) prepares your heart for His word. I believe that certain Patriarchs of the Bible lived such powerful lives because of the encounters and relationships they had with God. Abraham worshiped God, Moses had an experience of a burning bush and talked with God regularly, and David praised, thanked, and worshiped God regularly. We can see that they were fertile ground after their individual encounters with the Lord. Yet, even though we often study their end results, we sometimes forget where they started. Abraham, Moses and David all had places in their hearts that were not completely surrendered to the Lord early in their encounters with Him.

These un-surrendered places are called "strongholds" or "stony places". Each of them had stony places of distractions, temptation and persecution that needed to be given to God, so that they could manifest the reality of His presence and His purpose. God's promise is that He will remove the stone from out of our heart and give us a new heart. We just need to recognize the moments of temptation, prepare ourselves for the persecution and know how to respond. When we are drawn away, we should quickly repent, remember who (and whose) we are, and get back on track. All the while, we are to look to God who is the Author and Finisher of our faith.

> ***Ezekiel 36:25-27*** *NKJV*
>
> *25 Then I will sprinkle clean water on you, and you shall be clean; I will cleanse you from all your filthiness and from all your idols. 26 <u>I will give you a new heart</u> and put a new spirit within you; <u>I will take the heart of stone</u> out of your flesh <u>and give you a heart of flesh.</u> 27 I will put My Spirit within you and cause you to walk in My statutes, and you will keep My judgments and do them.*

When God is talking in Ezekiel 36:25-27, He's talking about *a new spirit that I will put within you, and a new heart I will give you.* He says, I'm going to take out that **stony** heart and I'm going to give you a heart of flesh. God had Ezekiel prophesy that He was going to remove from His children the stony (rocky) heart that will hardly produce and give His children a soft (pliable) heart that would walk in His statutes and in His ways. Notice, that before the stony heart is removed, He says He is going to sprinkle us clean with water (His word); to create a new soft and pliable heart. God was revealing the principles of the heart as well as the way that soil is produced (with water breaking down the rock - Ephesians 5:26).

I have found that when it is hard for me to surrender or give up an area completely to Jesus, I can pray and ask for His grace and strength to submit (it) to Him. He hears me when I reach out to Him in sincerity. With that grace, I receive strategy as well as strength to surrender, submit and release. Jesus will do the same for you because He is not a respecter of persons. This means, whoever reaches out in sincerity will have the same opportunity to receive. Do not get upset if a temptation has gotten the best of you. The inclination is to move from God when we fail, but we must do the opposite: Move closer to God, seek His forgiveness and know that He is a loving Father waiting with open arms ready to restore and accept you. His love never fails! He is always ready to hear you.

Enemy Strategy # 3: Cares of the world and the deceitfulness of riches

The third strategy of the enemy, according to the Matthew 13:22 is when the Sower sows the seeds among the thorns. The thorns represent the cares of the world and the deceitfulness of riches. These 'thorns' choke the seed (word) and the seed become unfruitful. Therefore, the heart does not produce.

> **Genesis 3:6** ^{KJV}
> ⁶ And when <u>the woman saw</u> that the <u>tree was good for food</u>, and that it was <u>pleasant to the eyes</u>, and a tree <u>to be desired to make one wise</u>, <u>she took</u> of the fruit thereof, and did eat, and gave also unto her husband with her; and he did eat.

The enemy painted such a vivid picture in Eve's mind that she became infatuated with the *possibilities* of a tree that she knew was forbidden. She became exposed to and drawn into the cares of the world, the pleasures of this life and the deceitfulness of riches. The problem is not the riches, but the *deceitfulness* (perception) of them and what they represent. The difference between you having them vs. them having you (you putting your trust in them). This is ultimately what caused God's word to be ejected from Adam and Eve's hearts. They saw more than the physical tree, they saw the deceit of the perceived possibilities which the enemy presented. Adam and Eve put their trust in what they could see outlined in Satan's picture and not in God's Picture (His instruction and wisdom).

> **Matthew 4:8-11** ^{KJV}
>
> *Again, the devil <u>taketh him</u> up into an <u>exceeding high mountain</u>, and <u>sheweth him all the kingdoms of the world, and the glory of them;</u> ⁹ And saith unto him, All these things will I give thee, if thou wilt fall down and worship me. ¹⁰ Then saith Jesus unto him, Get thee hence, Satan: for it is written, <u>Thou shalt worship the Lord thy God, and him only shalt thou serve.</u> ¹¹ Then the devil leaveth him, and, behold, angels came and ministered unto him.*

The devil really has no new ammunition. So, he tried the same method of operation (MO) with Jesus. He took Jesus to a high place so He could <u>see</u> real clear. He offered to give Jesus the kingdoms of the world (things that the world cares about) and the glory (glorious honor) of them. He painted an enticing picture…something that should get a King's attention (kingdoms and glory). He tried to entice Jesus by showing Him a glorious picture of something that He should want. Jesus understood that the way to the kingdom (of God) was not the path of least resistance but one that required forcefulness (He would later take it). He knew that if He bowed to the devil, He would become subject to him. Knowing His authority and being secure in His image, Jesus ordered the devil to get behind Him. He knew that soon the devil would be under His authority (His feet). Jesus protected His heart from the enemy and did not allow the devil to steal the word or the image of God from His heart. In the same manner and example of Jesus, it is important for you as a believer to know your authority, have confidence in your God-given image and take authority. You can tell the devil to get out of your face!

The devil knows that by getting you off focus he can win.

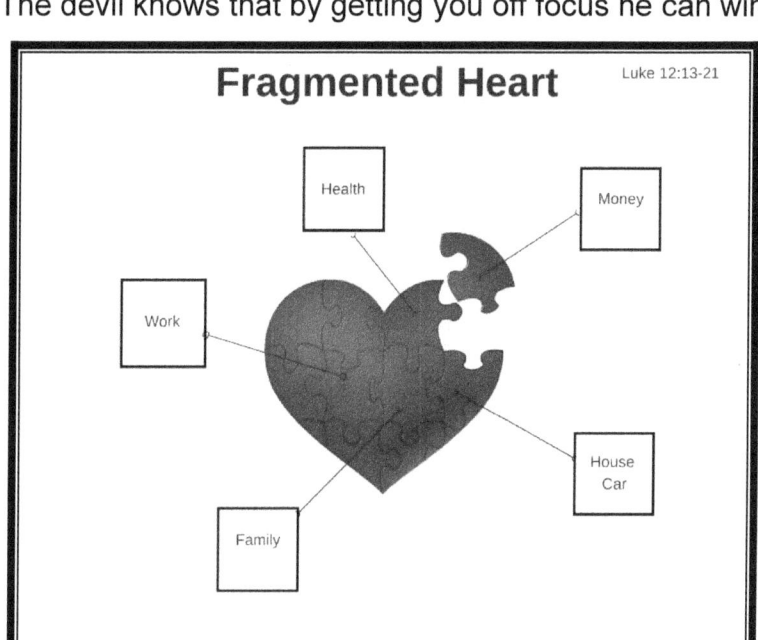

The devil desires that your heart be fragmented because a fragmented heart (ground) will not be able to operate in real power. When you're fragmented, your focus will be all over the place and you will not be able to produce. **Divided focus doesn't hit the target.** It leaves us open for destruction. The devil tries to use the same MO against us that he used against Jesus when they had the encounter in the wilderness. He hasn't changed the script at all. He will use doubt, temptation, the cares of this world (worry), the pleasures of this life, and the deceitfulness of riches to get the word of God and our rightful image out of our hearts. This is the reason that Jesus gives us the devil's playbook so we can be prepared and equipped to fight and win against him.

A word about division and unity
One day someone brought a man that was blind and couldn't talk to Jesus. We are told that in this instance this man was possessed by a demonic spirit. Jesus healed the man (exercised His authority) and a discussion soon broke out among the Pharisees that Jesus was casting out devils because He was working with the devil (basically they called him a devil). When Jesus found out what they were saying He taught them a very interesting lesson about division and unity...

> **Matthew 12:24-30** KJV
> [24] Now when the Pharisees heard it they said, "This fellow does not cast out demons except by Beelzebub, the ruler of the demons." [25] But Jesus knew their

> thoughts, and said to them: "Every kingdom divided against itself is brought to desolation, and every city or house divided against itself will not stand. ²⁶ If Satan casts out Satan, he is divided against himself. How then will his kingdom stand? ²⁷ And if I cast out demons by Beelzebub, by whom do your sons cast them out? Therefore they shall be your judges. ²⁸ But if I cast out demons by the Spirit of God, surely the kingdom of God has come upon you. ²⁹ Or how can one enter a strong man's house and plunder his goods, unless he first binds the strong man? And then he will plunder his house. ³⁰ He who is not with Me is against Me, and he who does not gather with Me scatters abroad.

Jesus explains to us in this passage that **a kingdom divided against itself cannot stand**. He breaks it down further and says a *city* divided against itself cannot stand. Yet, in a further step He declares that a *house* divided against itself cannot stand. What Jesus is letting us know is that without being unified we cannot stand; whether it is a kingdom, a country, a city or a home.

Let's look at this through an example of two people in a relationship. Let's say there is a nice young couple that has been dating for a few years, and they decide to get married. Inside of the groom are ideas and thoughts concerning fundamentals of their marriage that he's been 'married' to longer than he has known his fiancée. The bride has ideas and thoughts about marriage that she's had longer than she's known her fiancé. Then what happens, when they come together to marry with such divided ideas, is the potential for major conflict and clashes of epic proportions. This couple has to get to the place where their ideas are united so that their marriage will be productive. In other words, their marriage won't be divided and it will stand. Therefore, if a marriage is going to work we must choose to submit to one another *in the fear of the Lord*. When we allow our different ideologies to get between us, it often creates conflict and division and we ultimately fall apart. **There must be agreement on the fundamentals and foundation** so that there can be growth from that solid foundation.

The same is true for the Christian believer. As individuals, we usually have one set of thoughts and ideas that we have been living by before we come to God and have an encounter with Him. Then we become a part of God's family as a son or daughter. However, our thinking does not change. There are still un-surrendered and stony places and strongholds. The evidence of an unformed image of our new 'family' is that our behaviors and speech do not always line up with the King (His Word). The end result is division.

When we break the word *division* down, we have the word *"di"* which means *two*. Then the second part of the word is *"vision"* which means *single sight*. When there is a kingdom, city or house that has two visions the result is division, which will ultimately end up in di-vorce (two forces). When you have two visions in the house (marriage) you end up with two forces. Jesus says that two forces cannot stand (last). The structure will not stand. Two visions will divide a house. It cannot stand in a home, it cannot stand in a city or a government, and it cannot stand in the Kingdom of God. We see proof of that in what occurred with our enemy, Satan.

Satan at one time was an *anointed cherub* named Lucifer, who was created by God with a function of providing music (Ezekiel 28:14). He had a place within the Kingdom of God. One day he developed a mindset that did not line up with God's vision. His vision of himself became grander than what his position was in the plan of God. He thought of usurping God's place, thinking, *"I am beautiful, I can sing, I will ascend into the heavens, I will be like the most high God"* (Isaiah 14:13-14). Before he could almost finish the thought, BAM!! – like lightning, Satan fell from heaven (Luke 10:18). It did not take long at all. Michael, the archangel, dealt very swiftly with the enemy and threw him out of the kingdom (Revelations 12:7-9).

God understands that **division brings death to any kingdom** and He deals with it swiftly. On top of kicking Satan out of the heavens – to add insult to injury – God decided that He was going to make man rule over Satan! So God decided to create this creature in His image (mankind) that is so much like He is, that Satan is going to see God in man (man in God) and fear them. God's divine purpose is for man (male and female) to keep him (Satan) in his place (with the authority that He gave them) and to rule over him. In order for this to happen, man must make the **Kingdom of God the highest priority**.

Whole Heart
Matthew 6:33

Seek first the Kingdom of God

God & His Word

Family | Work

Health | Money | House Car

You cannot seek first the kingdom without first seeking the King (God). When you do this, everything else falls into the correct order and the King can now lead you properly in your affairs. In this order, your thoughts are aligned with the King and you are now unified. Satan knows that when you operate with the King's Word in your heart, you will wreak havoc upon his kingdom and *occupy*. You will take control and no longer be passive in life.

Part 3

Kingdom Domination

Chapter 5

Kingdom Thinking

Thinking Like The King

Jesus was often asked a lot of questions by the religious leaders who were trying to trap Him in His words. For example, the Pharisees and the Sadducees wanted to discredit Him. Their hearts were hard and they didn't like what He was doing. After all, He was drawing attention away from them. In this instance below, the Pharisees questioned Jesus concerning divorce...

> **Mathew 19:3-8** NKJV
>
> *The Pharisees also came to Him, testing Him, and saying to Him, "Is it lawful for a man to divorce his wife for just any reason?" ⁴ And He answered and said to them, "Have you not read that He who made them at the beginning 'made them male and female,' ⁵ and said, 'For this reason a man shall leave his father and mother and be joined to his wife, and the two shall become one flesh'? ⁶ So then, they are no longer two but one flesh. Therefore what God has joined together, let not man separate." ⁷ They said to Him, "Why then did Moses command to give a certificate of divorce, and to put her away?" ⁸ He said to them, "Moses, because of the hardness of your hearts, permitted you to divorce your wives, but from the beginning it was not so.*

Note Jesus' response in verse 8: *"He said unto them, Moses because of the hardness of your hearts, permitted you to divorce your wives,* **but from the beginning it was not so.**" Jesus' basically said, Listen I don't care what the *popular belief is or what society has voted on. My reference point (for any answer) is what was established* **at the beginning**.*"* Or, another way of saying it is, *I see everything the way God sees it and intended for things to function from the beginning.* With that being said, when God thinks of you His reference point is <u>from the beginning</u>. He sees how you were created to function from the beginning.

Let's take a look at what God sees when He sees us:

> **Genesis 1:26-28** ^{NKJV}
>
> [26] Then God said, "Let Us make man in Our image, according to Our likeness; let them have dominion over the fish of the sea, over the birds of the air, and over the cattle, over all the earth and over every creeping thing that creeps on the earth." [27] So God created man in His own image; in the image of God He created him; male and female He created them. [28] Then God blessed them, and God said to them, "Be fruitful and multiply; fill the earth and subdue it; have dominion over the fish of the sea, over the birds of the air, and over every living thing that moves on the earth."

God tells us, at the beginning, that He made man (mankind, male and female) in His image and in His likeness. Since He has made *man* in His image and His likeness, this means that there is a part of man that is *just like God!* God is all-powerful and He has all-dominion. So how could He then create mankind (you) without giving you power and dominion? It's not possible. The purpose of God creating mankind and putting them on the Earth was to give His creation dominion and for mankind to subdue the Earth. That means that your original purpose *from the beginning* was to have dominion over every situation and every circumstance that you would encounter. Every single one! We have a God-given right to dominion: to dominate in Christ and to exercise that dominion. If you would start to view every obstacle in your life as an opportunity to dominate and overcome, rather than as drudgery, you would develop the proper Kingdom (of God) mindset that God intended for you to possess in the beginning!

<u>Dominion</u> means the exercise of power over a domain. Man's domain is the Earth. God is in Heaven and He has delegated man on Earth to exercise His (God's) influence on Earth. He's exercising His dominion from Heaven through us. What God wants is for His perfect will; His Word, His truth -- to be worked out through His man (men and women) that He has created here on Earth. This was, and still is His plan from the beginning.

Subdue means to conquer, to bring into subjection and to have control or influence over. God's intent was for man to conquer, and have all things under control. We are to make our situations and circumstances come under our control and to be subject to us, our words and our decree. This is the will of God.

Authority means the power to influence or to command. You were created with this power (authority) already on the inside of you. It is through submission that authority is really understood. If you understand authority, you understand that you must be told what to do (this is submission). Here is a powerful example of authority and faith based on submission...

> ***Luke 7:2-9*** *NKJV*
> *² And a certain centurion's servant, who was dear to him, was sick and ready to die. ³ So when he heard about Jesus, he sent elders of the Jews to Him, pleading with Him to come and heal his servant. ⁴ And when they came to Jesus, they begged Him earnestly, saying that the one for whom He should do this was deserving, ⁵ "for he loves our nation, and has built us a synagogue." ⁶ Then Jesus went with them. And when He was already not far from the house, the centurion sent friends to Him, saying to Him, "Lord, do not trouble Yourself, for I am not worthy that You should enter*

under my roof. ⁷ Therefore I did not even think myself worthy to come to You. But say the word, and my servant will be healed. ⁸ For I also am a man placed under authority, having soldiers under me. And I say to one, 'Go,' and he goes; and to another, 'Come,' and he comes; and to my servant, 'Do this,' and he does it." ⁹ When Jesus heard these things, He marveled at him, and turned around and said to the crowd that followed Him, "I say to you, I have not found such great faith, not even in Israel!"

The centurion soldier said, in verse 8: *"For I also am a man placed under authority, having soldiers under me. And I say to one, 'Go,' and he goes; and to another, 'Come,' and he comes; and to my servant, 'Do this,' and he does it."* He was basically saying, *'I understand the principles, Jesus, just speak a word over my current situation. I understand that when I speak, things take place and orders are followed. Therefore, since I can see that You have authority, You just need to speak and I know that things go into motion and happen.'* I also would like to point out that this centurion soldier said that he was a man <u>under</u> authority. He understood that just like he listens when commands are made, he has those who listen to him when he commands. In other words, *it is measured back to him the way that he measures* (Matthew 7:2). This is the example of Kingdom thinking that man was intended to have *from the beginning.* This is what God expects of us. We are told what to do and we respond accordingly. Likewise, we tell things what to do and they respond accordingly.

It is plain to see that God wanted his man and woman to rule, reign and to control everything that concerned them. This is how it was from the beginning and this is how it is supposed to be now. Jesus ruled every circumstance and the people marveled at the things that He did. But in truth, we are supposed to do the very same thing. There should not be one thing that we are <u>under</u>. Sickness, disease, pain, hurt, financial struggle, and the list goes on, are all supposed to be <u>under</u> our control. Jesus died so that the blessing would reside on, in and around us. We are blessed, and what God has blessed cannot be cursed (*Numbers 23*). As a Kingdom resident, you have been reinstated to your place of dominion, strength and authority and the gates of hell cannot prevail against you! You are *more than* a conqueror, and He that lives in you is greater than any evil wicked device of the enemy. You rule and you reign. That is your design from the beginning and that is your end!

> **Psalm 8:3-6** [NKJV]
>
> *When I consider Your heavens, the work of Your fingers, The moon and the stars, which You have ordained,* ⁴ *What is man that You are mindful of him,*

And the son of man that You visit him? ⁵ For You have made him a little lower than the angels, And You have crowned him with glory and honor. ⁶ You have made him to have dominion over the works of Your hands; You have put all things under his feet,

In this verse the word 'angels' is not in the original translation. The original word is "Elohim", which means God. This is how the scripture should read: *"You have made him a little lower than God, And You have crowned him with glory and honor. ⁶ <u>You have made him to have dominion</u> over the works of Your hands.*

This is your purpose as a Kingdom resident. When you create something, your original intent is its purpose. God said that **He created us to have dominion.** So your purpose is now being revealed to you through Scripture. Scripture is God's words and His thoughts. I would just like to clear up a point here before someone gets confused...<u>We were not created to dominate each other and we are not God Almighty</u>.

> **Romans 5:17** ᴺᴷᴶⱽ (talking about Adam's sin in the garden) says: *For if by the one man's offense death reigned through the one, much more those who receive abundance of grace and of the gift of righteousness will reign in life through the One, Jesus Christ.*

The scripture is saying that we should be reigning in life right now...currently. We're supposed to reign in every area of our life. Paul is saying, if you receive the abundance of grace that Christ died on the cross for you to have, if you receive the gift of righteousness that Christ died on the cross for you to have, then you reign in this life by The One—Jesus Christ. This is not to say that nothing will go wrong in your life and that you will live a happy go-lucky life every day without obstacles. Reigning and dominating in life is a Kingdom mindset that says you will not live under your circumstances but live above them.

What are you really?

Would you be surprised if Jesus said that you are a god? As I clarified previously, you are <u>not</u> God Almighty. However, you are a god. One day, Jesus was talking and the Pharisees and the Sadducees became so upset with what He was saying that they wanted to stone Him. Jesus' response was, "For what good work do you stone Me?"

> *John 10:31-36 NKJV*
> *31 Then the Jews took up stones again to stone Him. 32 Jesus answered them, "Many good works I have shown you from My Father. For which of those works do you stone Me?" 33 The Jews answered Him, saying, "For a good work we do not stone You, but for blasphemy,*

> *and because You, being a Man, make Yourself God."* ³⁴ *Jesus answered them, "Is it not written in your law, 'I said, "You are gods"'?* ³⁵ *If He called them gods, to whom the word of God came (and the Scripture cannot be broken),* ³⁶ *do you say of Him whom the Father sanctified and sent into the world, 'You are blaspheming,' because I said, 'I am the Son of God'?*

Now do you see this? Jesus says that we are gods (v34) (not deity, but small 'g'). These are two differing perspectives. The Jews were thinking and talking about tradition. Jesus was talking about relationship with the Father. Jesus equated Himself so much with God that they got angry with Him. Traditions will tell you that you cannot equate yourself with God. However, a relationship with God will tell you, you can understand yourself to be a god. After all, Jesus' message of the Kingdom of God was about God's Spirit (Christ in you, the hope of glory (Colossians1:27)).

So when it comes to your domain – which is your household, business, finances, personal purpose, and your life overall, you are the g-o-d and you should reign. Christ – in you – is the hope (assurance) of your dominion. Without this mindset it will be difficult to dominate and reign in life as God intended for you. Remember…it was decreed at the beginning.

Chapter 6

Kingdom Image

Image of God

> #### Genesis 1:26-27 KJV
>
> ²⁶ *And God said, Let us make man in our image, after our likeness: and let them have dominion over the fish of the sea, and over the fowl of the air, and over the cattle, and over all the earth, and over every creeping thing that creepeth upon the earth.* ²⁷ *So God created man in his own image, in the image of God created he him; male and female created he them.*

The very first thing that God gave to man (mankind) was not dominion, it was image. Therefore, if you try to dominate with the wrong image, it's not going to work out for you. The Word is our mirror by which we get to see <u>how</u> we are like Him. God gave us His image and made us like Him. *We are like Him! What an amazing image!* You are more than a conqueror; you are fearfully and wonderfully made. You are so intricate that you can't even figure yourself out. **We need God's word to reveal to us who we are.** God gave us His image and then He says, "I'm going to give you dominion, rule and reign over all the Earth". Everyone should have a sphere of influence and a place where we call our domain. This is the place where we are supposed to be ruling and reigning in life. God's Word (His thoughts) is here to reveal to us how. We know that man fell from the place of authority (Gen. 3). They (Adam and Eve) listened to the devil, and they fell (When I mention man, I'm talking about mankind - the human race, because He created us, male and female (Gen.1:27)).

In the following scripture from Mark 12, Jesus is talking about something natural, but there is a spiritual concept that He also wants us to receive.

> **Mark 12:13-14** ^{KJV}
>
> *^{13} And they send unto him certain of the Pharisees and of the Herodians, to catch him in his words. ^{14} And when they were come, they say unto him, Master, we know that thou art true, and carest for no man: for thou regardest not the person of men, but teachest the way of God in truth: Is it lawful to give tribute to Caesar, or not?*

The Pharisees and Herodians were trying to trap Jesus in His own words. They wanted Jesus to say '*no*', so that they could go to the Roman Empire and accuse Jesus before the officials and say He was not going to pay His taxes.

> **Mark 12:15-17** ^{KJV}
>
> *^{15} Shall we give, or shall we not give? But he, knowing their hypocrisy, said unto them, Why tempt ye me? bring me a penny, that I may see it. ^{16} And they brought it. And he saith unto them,* **Whose is this image** *and*

superscription? And they said unto him, Caesar's. ¹⁷ And Jesus answering said unto them, Render to Caesar the things that are Caesar's, and to God the things that are God's. And they marvelled at him.

I want you to see this from a spiritual perspective, because I believe that a lot of us are walking around carrying and holding on to images that are not like God. Jesus is saying we should give the things that belong to God to God. You're created in God's image, so *you give yourself to God*. While they were trying to capture Him in His words, Jesus was saying, *look...this image is not you, why are you so worried about this external image?* I believe that we should only concern ourselves with the image of who we are in Him and from Him.

When we allow images that are not like God's image to enter our minds and become our reality, those images will begin to dictate thoughts, speech and behavior that are contrary to God's purpose. Our end result will be a malfunction. The wrong image allowed to reside on the inside of you will begin to rule and reign over you when you should be ruling and reigning over it. When we are not aligned with the Word of God we become somewhat like a donkey, with a carrot in front of it: We look at and follow external enticements - trying to capture things when we can attract them. **We should take more time to**

consider who we are, really. That type of focus will bring about a God-ordained change in our life and outcomes. Instead of following after things, we will be able to attract them to us. We will be amazed at the life that we produce from this continual practice.

The Power of the Imagination

Let's discuss the power of imagination as we review Genesis chapter 6.

> *Genesis 6:5-6* ^{KJV}
> *⁵ And God saw that the wickedness of man was great in the earth, and that **every imagination** of the **thoughts of his heart** was only evil continually. ⁶ And it repented the Lord that he had made man on the earth, and it grieved him at his heart.*

When God first created everything, He said everything was good (Gen 1:31). Then we see in Genesis 6:5-6 where, when the image changed on the inside of man, it grieved God in His heart because it was wickedness. What was once good now became wickedness. When man fell, they lost more than their authority: They lost their image. Image gave man their identity, which caused them to walk in their authority. The word 'imagination' in Hebrew is 'yester', which means a framed thing, framework and form.

The word 'thought' in Hebrew means 'texture, plan or intention'. **A thought is a texture.** Think about a thought this way; it is captured in our imagination (framework) which is located in our spiritual heart. So when the texture (thought) is framed in our imagination, we begin to see it in our minds. This is how powerful our imaginations are: We actually begin to 'see' the thought, not with our physical eyes; I mean we can close our eyes and still see it. Captured thoughts become a textured thing in our minds. It takes form, the longer we focus on it. So, the principle of focus shows us that what we begin to focus on subconsciously develops until we begin to attract it, in the same way that a magnet is attracted to metal. Keeping this in mind, let's look at Hebrews...

> **Hebrews 11:1-3** KJV
>
> *¹Now **faith** is the **substance** of things hoped for, the evidence of things not seen. ² For by it the elders obtained a good report. ³ Through **faith** we understand that the worlds were **framed** by the **word of God**, so that things which are seen were **not made of things which do appear**.*

Let me break it down for you. When God says that the Earth was void and dark (Gen 1:2), He had a vision in his mind of how light looked. He framed light in His imagination and spoke saying, "Light be," and light came forth. **Light knew what to be because God had an internal picture of it before He spoke it into existence.** Here is a question for you... How would God know what light was if He didn't have a picture of it before He spoke it? I believe this lets us know that before God spoke anything, He took a texture, or thought in His imagination and then expressed it by His words and it came to pass. A God with this power and wisdom, Who created and framed the things that we can and cannot see says, "I've created man in my own image, so that man will operate just like I operate."

In the Old Testament, God wanted to move his chosen people into the Promised Land that He had prepared for them. However, with the wrong image it was very challenging. There is a cost of having the wrong Image.

> ***Numbers 13:1-2; 17-21; 25-33*** *KJV*
> *[1] And the Lord spake unto Moses, saying, [2] Send thou men, that they may search the land of Canaan, which I give unto the children of Israel: of every tribe of their fathers shall ye send a man, everyone a ruler among them. [17] And Moses sent them to spy out the land of Canaan, and said unto them, Get you up this way southward, and go up into the mountain: [18] And see the land, what it is, and the people that dwelleth therein, whether they be strong or weak, few or many; [19] And*

what the land is that they dwell in, whether it be good or bad; and what cities they be that they dwell in, whether in tents, or in strong holds; [20] And what the land is, whether it be fat or lean, whether there be wood therein, or not. And be ye of good courage, and bring of the fruit of the land. Now the time was the time of the firstripe grapes. [21] So they went up, and searched the land…[25] And they returned from searching of the land after forty days. [26] And they went and came to Moses, and to Aaron, and to all the congregation of the children of Israel, unto the wilderness of Paran, to Kadesh; and brought back word unto them, and unto all the congregation, and shewed them the fruit of the land. [27] And they told him, and said, We came unto the land whither thou sentest us, and surely it floweth with milk and honey; and this is the fruit of it. [28] Nevertheless the people be strong that dwell in the land, and the cities are walled, and very great: and moreover we saw the children of Anak there. [29] The Amalekites dwell in the land of the south: and the Hittites, and the Jebusites, and the Amorites, dwell in the mountains: and the Canaanites dwell by the sea, and by the coast of Jordan. [30] And Caleb stilled the people before Moses, and said, Let us go up at once, and possess it; for we are well able to overcome it. [31] But the men that went up with him said, We be not able to go up against the people; for they are stronger than we. [32] And they brought up an evil report of the land which they had searched unto the children of Israel, saying, The land, *through which we have gone to search it, is a land that eateth up the inhabitants thereof; and all the people that we saw in it are men of a great stature. ³³ And there we saw the giants, the sons of Anak, which come of the giants: and **we were in our own sight** as grasshoppers, and so we were **in their sight**.*

Numbers 14:1-4 ᴷᴶⱽ
*¹And all the congregation lifted up their voice, and cried; and the people wept that night. ² And all the children of Israel murmured against Moses and against Aaron: and the whole congregation said unto them, Would God that we had died in the land of Egypt! or would God we had died in this wilderness! ³ And wherefore hath the Lord brought us unto this land, to fall by the sword, that our wives and our children should be a prey? were it not **better for us to return into Egypt?** ⁴ And they said one to another, Let us make a captain, and **let us return into Egypt**.*

God led the Children of Israel out of Egypt with Moses leading them. This was supposed to be a transition period; it was only supposed to last for a few days. God wanted them to come out of Egypt to worship Him and then He was going to lead them into the Promised Land. Instead, they were not able to draw near to Him because the image they had of Him frightened them (Exodus 20:18-21). However, Moses who was a man just like them, but with a different image inside, wanted to draw nearer to God when He revealed Himself. Meanwhile, the Israelites were wondering, how are we going to get into the Promise Land? Just like many of us, the Israelites did not understand that God already had a plan. He was going to send in some insects into the land and chase out all of the inhabitants, but they couldn't see it.

Note: When you go into the wilderness, which represents a transition period or a time of testing (trials and temptations), there are two ways out.

1. After you step in, you can step back to where you were.
2. You can go through to the other side (where the promises are).

What you do is determined by what you see spiritually and naturally. The children of Israel wanted to go back because they had images of what they had left back in Egypt (Exodus 16:3). Even though they were slaves and in bondage in Egypt, at least they could sit around the pots and eat. They were mistreated, whipped and forced to labor and build for the Egyptians. Yet, somehow in their minds they were better off in bondage than free. They did not have the heart, power and the wherewithal to get across to the other side. So they wanted to go back, because their internal image had not changed. **You can only move forward when the internal image changes for the positive**.

Just like the children of Israel, some of us are carrying images of the past and yet we are still trying to move forward. That would be like me driving on I-95 south highway with my head looking north (backward). How far do you think I would get before I would wreck? Allowing ourselves to focus on the images from our pasts keeps us from moving forward and making progress. I am sympathetic when it comes to what others have suffered through in their past because I know a lot of people (myself included) have been through some very difficult times. I am not trying to make light of life's trials, experiences and difficulties. It is simply my conviction that the blood of Jesus is able to cover it. It is the blood of Jesus that covers our sins and puts them in the sea of forgetfulness. Please don't discount what the blood has done for you, for me and all those who have accepted Christ's work on the cross at Calvary. Jesus did more than just die so we can get to heaven when we die. The devil wants you to think that is all you get. However, when Jesus died for us, He also rose up. Ephesians 2:6 says that *He raised us up together to sit with him in heavenly places in Christ Jesus.*

If you look at Ephesians 1:20-23, it tells us where He is seated: far above all principality, power, might, dominion and any name that is named. **You sit right there with Him because you were built to rule and to reign!** We were not built or designed to have situations and circumstances get the best of us. Situations and circumstances are supposed to be under our feet. Yes, it can be difficult. Yes, it can be rough. Even though some of our past encounters have left us hurt, discouraged and rejected, believe and receive that we are stronger because we made it through. The purpose of difficulties is to try to distract us, but God is saying, "You were meant to rule and to reign over the situation and the circumstances". Utilize the difficulties as lessons to become stronger. So don't look backward to where you were, and don't get caught up in where you are right now. There is a shift that has to take place, where what you see internally shifts into a place that overrides the negativity and pain of the past and present. That shift is what propels you forward. You have to *focus forward*, and look at something different and expect a better and different outcome. This will keep you moving forward and you are going to get through to the other side. Don't stop. You can do it. You were built and designed for forward movement and success.

There is one more ingredient that we will have to discuss before moving on – which is Faith, and getting it to work in our lives. If we are going to rule and reign in our lives, we will need faith. In order to have strong faith we will need to understand the Belief Cycle. The Belief Cycle consist of words, thoughts, images, expectations, faith and experiences.

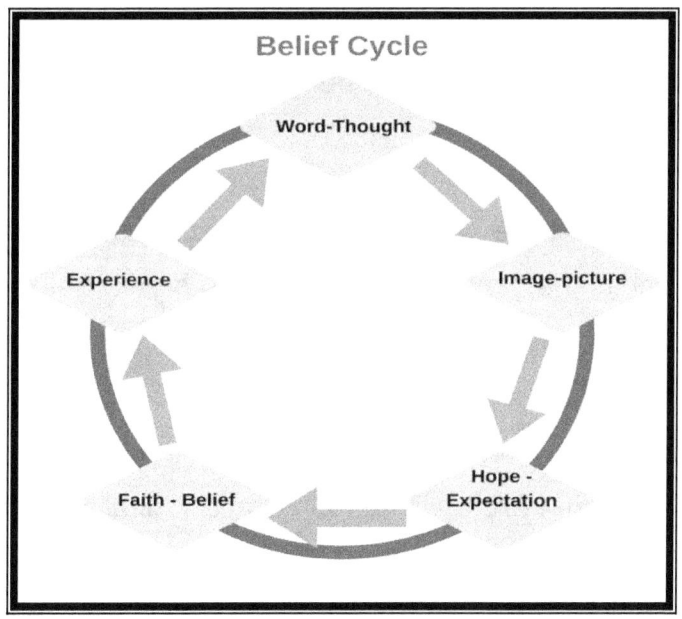

Faith and the Belief Cycle

The belief cycle works like this: You have a word or a thought which creates a picture or an image; a textured thing framed in your imagination. This textured thing in turn creates a hope and an expectation. Your expectation will determine what you believe. Note the intersection between belief and faith. Faith jumps in and says, 'I'm going to speak or somehow <u>take action</u> in what I believe'. From that cycle and interaction, you now have an experience, and then the whole cycle repeats itself again, based on your experience. So, belief is the foundation and faith is the catalyst, the movement and the predecessor of the realization of the image being made real.

Changing the Belief System

If you are like me, you may have some beliefs, behaviors and habits that you are finding hard to break. But there is good news. Your belief system can be changed. I am changing mine right now. I realized that there were areas of my life that I had not made progress in because I have had limiting beliefs. The more that I challenge these limiting beliefs...the more I see them changing. As a consequence, there are areas of my life that are changing as well.

[d] Bob Harrison, who mentored me through his work years ago, is a well-known speaker and author in the area of

financial increase. He said that he felt guilty that he was making so much money. He also said that he had to actually get into the Word of God and study in order to change his way of thinking. He did what was called a BMW: a Behavior Modification Workshop. It's not actually something that you buy. It's something that you do. Bob saturated himself with information on increase. He listened to the word of God concerning finances continuously. He had audio CDs and tapes (it was the pre-digital age) he listened to it in every bathroom at his house. Also, when he was in the car, or walking around with headphones on, he would listen to teachings on increase. All that he listened to was regarding increase. Bob no longer began to feel guilty about making money because he now believed that it was God's will for him to be prosperous.

The reason that he felt guilty about making money was probably because of something that he was taught growing up. To erase the wrong thinking about money he had to hear something different and it had to be enough to override the old thinking. You and I are built the same way. We will have to select what we will allow to grow in the soil of our heart. In the process, we may probably have to unlearn some things.

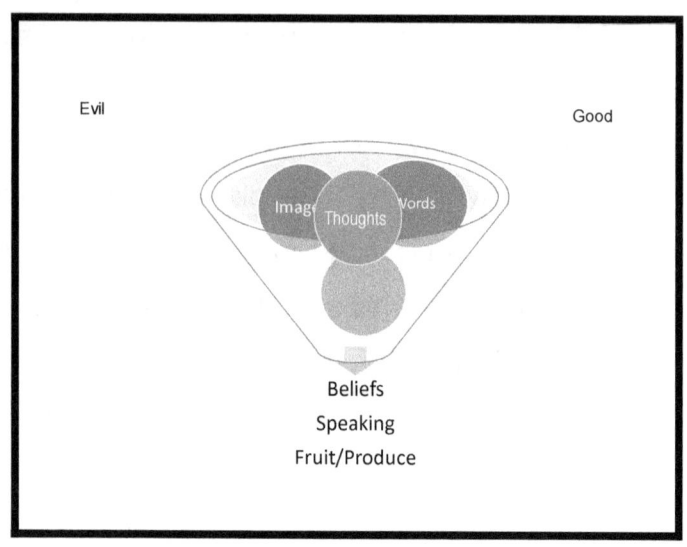

Images, Thoughts & Words = what you believe, speak and produce (behavior).

Fear works the same way. That's why you have to guard your heart and mouth. 1) You speak and you take action on what you have come to believe 2) You have an experience 3) You repeat the cycle all over again. Now, all of this usually happens without any conscious awareness, so it operates on a subconscious level. Have you ever driven someplace and wondered how you got there? It's like you daydreamed the whole way there and didn't even remember the journey? Has this happened to you – have you arrived at some place in your life, and you're not even sure how you got there? You don't even realize it (which is why this concept is so powerful). This process is going on, all of the time. It's constant. With the repetition of thoughts and actions, a groove gets developed. Think of how a CD plays your song when you hit 'play', and compare it to when you hit 'play' and your thoughts begin to play, and your behavior coincides. When thoughts and behavior play out together, then habits are created. So now you operate out of something habitual, over and over again, because that's how our brains were designed to learn. This is a good thing when the information is good, but it can be a bad thing when the information you input is wrong.

A huge key to understanding your belief system is that your recurring dominant thoughts will equal your ways or behavior. Your dominant thought patterns are going to be equivalent to what you do and say. Whatever you think about the most you're going to draw to you. It really is a "Law of Attraction". Jesus put it this way…

> **Matthew 5:28** *NKJV But I say to you that whoever looks at a woman to lust for her has already committed adultery with her in his heart.*

This is how powerful your imagination is. Jesus said, if you are a man or a woman and you think about another woman or man in a certain way in your imagination, it's counted as if you committed the act.

Limiting Limitations

The process of training some circus elephants involves their trainers taking a baby elephant, wrapping a chain around its leg, then putting a stake in the ground and tying the chain to it. When the baby elephant tries to pull away from the stake, it's to no avail. It cannot pull away. The stake and chain limits their movement. Elephants are known for their amazing memory. So, fast-forward many years and the elephant has grown up into adulthood. You have this big, huge creature with enormous strength that can easily yank this stake out of the ground. However, the elephant's mind is saying, "I can't do it because I tried and tried when I was younger and it didn't work." This mind-control on the elephant contains them and keeps them in a place of powerlessness. This big, enormous, powerful creature that God created has a little area that it can barely move around in. It does this because of previous experiences of powerlessness.

> ***Romans 8.11*** *NKJV*
> *[11] But if the Spirit of Him who raised Jesus from the dead dwells in you, He who raised Christ from the dead will also give life to your mortal bodies through His Spirit who dwells in you.*

We are also God's creation; enormous (on the inside) with His power, anointing and with His Spirit. However, if we don't have the right image of God on the inside we will have a limited expectation of our lives, while we have a God who is limitless.

Another trick of the devil is to make you think that you're not powerful. If he can make you think you're not powerful, he can keep you in your place. You don't really have 'a place' because God has designed you to be powerful like He is. However, if the devil can convince you otherwise, then he will convince you that you have limits. That's the whole reason that Egypt put Israel in bondage; the Israelites were multiplying rapidly, and the Egyptians were afraid that the Israelites were going to outnumber and overpower them (Exodus 1:8-11). Pharaoh used the strategy of fear to put the Israelites in bondage in the same way that the devil uses fear as a strategy against Christians. He knows that fear and experiences of powerlessness will create limits and keep the Christian in a limited space — much like the elephant trainer does with the elephant. God however has a different plan for His Kingdom people. He plans for His church (the called out ones) to walk in their God-given ability and to exercise their godly dominion over the kingdom of darkness.

Unifying with God's Word
Words create thoughts and your thoughts create words

and behavior. So, in order to change your belief cycle you must inject different thoughts into your mind through a process of repetition and faith and belief. The process should be continual and eventually affect our subconscious. God wants to get the correct image into us. We have and utilize the Word of God, because it is God's thoughts. Having His word in us will create or put the correct image in us. We have to become one (unified) with His word (in our thinking and behavior) in order for the word to work in our lives and to walk in the full Kingdom authority that God has given to us.

Chapter 7

Seeing It

Your Image + Authority = Domination

In 1 Samuel 17 there was someone who understood what it meant to have God's image and authority. This person was David. The Philistines gathered their armies together to fight against the Israeli army. The Philistines had moved into Judah's territory and they had taken something that belonged to the Israelites (God's promise). The Philistines were on one mountain and Israel was on the other mountain, with a valley in between them. Each day, they would put the battle into array, but no one fought. There was just a lot of talking going on – mostly on the side of the Philistines.

> ***1 Samuel 17:4-11*** *KJV*
> *⁴ And there went out a champion out of the camp of the Philistines, named Goliath, of Gath, whose height was six cubits and a span. ⁵ And he had an helmet of brass upon his head, and he was armed with a coat of mail; and the weight of the coat was five thousand shekels of brass. ⁶ And he had greaves of brass upon his legs, and a target of brass between his shoulders. ⁷ And the staff of his spear was like a weaver's beam; and his spear's head weighed six hundred shekels of iron: and one bearing a shield went before him. ⁸ And he stood and cried unto the armies of Israel, and said unto them, Why are ye come out to set your battle in array? am not I a Philistine, and ye servants to Saul? choose you a man for you, and let him come down to me. ⁹ If he be able to*

> fight with me, and to kill me, then will we be your servants: but if I prevail against him, and kill him, then shall ye be our servants, and serve us. ¹⁰ And the Philistine said, I defy the armies of Israel this day; give me a man, that we may fight together. ¹¹ When Saul and all Israel heard those words of the Philistine, they were dismayed, and greatly afraid.

The Israeli army and the king were intimidated and they shrunk back into despair and fear upon seeing this giant and hearing his words of mocking every day. **Fear causes you to shrink back, while faith causes you to press forward.** There didn't seem to be anyone who could, or was willing to fight the giant. So the situation continued. The giant was fully dressed and he was bullying them with a seemingly impossible situation. Their internal image was very small in the face of this (literal) giant problem!

> **1 Samuel 17:16** ^{KJV}
> ¹⁶ And the Philistine drew near morning and evening, and presented himself forty days.

For forty days...morning and evening, the giant said the same thing. That's at least eighty times! *He actually made them <u>meditate on his word</u>.* **The enemy will do that; he will speak mess to you daily, if he is given the chance.**

Three of David's brothers served in the Israeli army, so they were hearing and seeing the same thing for forty days (v13). Meanwhile, David was back in the fields feeding the sheep (v15). Prior to this battle David had been with Saul (the King) playing music for him, because Saul had an evil spirit on him (1 Samuel 16:14, 17, 23). David's dad (Jesse) called David in from the field to take some food down to the captain of a thousand. Jesse's strategy was that he was trying to take care of the captain so that his sons weren't put on the front line. (Jesse was a smart man, indeed!)

> ***1 Samuel 17:20-24*** *KJV*
> *[20] And David rose up early in the morning, and left the sheep with a keeper, and took, and went, as Jesse had commanded him; and he came to the trench, as the host was going forth to the fight, and shouted for the battle. [21] For Israel and the Philistines had put the battle in array, army against army. [22] And David left his carriage in the hand of the keeper of the carriage, and ran into the army, and came and saluted his brethren. [23] And as he talked with them, behold, there came up the champion, the Philistine of Gath, Goliath by name, out of the armies of the Philistines, and spake according to the same words: and David heard them [24] And all the men of Israel, when they saw the man, fled from him, and were sore afraid.*

David heard the same words that the Israeli army had been hearing for forty days. Yet, instead of being intimidated, David had courage. He saw things differently. He had faith. He didn't even care about what the giant was saying. He had been out with the sheep, and he'd been praising God with his harp and singing songs to the Lord. **Worship and the presence of God can make you impervious to outside forces and information.** He had something different on the inside of him.

David had an image created by being in the Presence of God. He could hear words that were disturbing and not be disturbed, because those words didn't change what he had on the inside. David knew who he was and the prior battles he had fought and had won. David spoke with assurance. He wanted to know what would be given to him when he defeated the giant. They told him the person who defeated Goliath would get the king's daughter and their father's house would be free of taxes (1 Samuel 17:25-27). *Now, that's a good deal*! No one in the army spoke the way David spoke, so his words got back to Saul (v31). (Hey Saul, there's somebody that wants to fight this giant.) **Your faith filled words will do the same thing. They will be rehearsed before the KING (Jesus).** Your words will get the attention of someone who is in a position to advance you and show you favor.

1 Samuel 17:31-33 KJV

³¹ And when the words were heard which David spake, they rehearsed them before Saul: and he sent for him. ³² And David said to Saul, Let no man's heart fail because of him; thy servant will go and fight with this Philistine. ³³ And Saul said to David, Thou art not able to go against this Philistine to fight with him: for thou art but a youth, and he a man of war from his youth.

There will always be people that try to tell you what you can and can't do, can and can't win, and so on. These are the crushers of the dream. David's own brother (a crusher/hater) tried to get him to focus on the sheep that he was watching (1 Samuel 17:28), and now the king was trying to tell him that he had no experience! Crushers and haters are all around and will focus on your inexperience and assumed inability.

This is what you have to do. *You have to remind yourself of the past victories that God has brought you through.* If you don't remind yourself of what you've gone through and how you've overcome, then you're going to fall back on an image that is not yours. If this was David's case he would have been just like everybody else. That is why he corrected Saul and said these words...

1 Samuel 17:34-37 *KJV*

³⁴ And David said unto Saul, Thy servant kept his father's sheep, and there came a lion, and a bear, and took a lamb out of the flock: ³⁵ And I went out after him, and smote him, and delivered it out of his mouth: and when he arose against me, I caught him by his beard, and smote him, and slew him. ³⁶ Thy servant slew both the lion and the bear: and this uncircumcised Philistine shall be as one of them, seeing he hath defied the armies of the living God. ³⁷ David said moreover, The Lord that delivered me out of the paw of the lion, and out of the paw of the bear, he will deliver me out of the hand of this Philistine. And Saul said unto David, Go, and the Lord be with thee.

David decided to move. He took action. We know he was in faith because *he spoke something*, and he was also prepared to back it up with actions! Faith requires some type of movement. **Your faith is going to require that you take action: Action with your words and action with your hands.**

Proverbs 12:14 *NIV ¹⁴ From the fruit of their lips people are filled with good things, and the work of their hands brings them reward.*

1 Samuel 17:38-40 *KJV*

³⁸ And Saul armed David with his armour, and he put a

helmet of brass upon his head; also he armed him with a coat of mail. ³⁹ And David girded his sword upon his armour, and he assayed to go; for he had not proved it. And David said unto Saul, I cannot go with these; for I have not proved them. And David put them off him.⁴⁰ And he took his staff in his hand, and chose him five smooth stones out of the brook, and put them in a shepherd's bag which he had, even in a scrip; and his sling was in his hand: and he drew near to the Philistine.

I want you to visualize what David was wearing. He may have seemed to be improperly dressed for the battle that he was about to fight. Saul was trying to equip David in the way that he thought he would be successful. **People will want you to conform to what they are used to.** Saul had armor that was used in battle and so did Goliath. *Just because people aren't used to the way that you do things does not mean that it is wrong.* David's fight was with the Philistine, yet so far he had to fight:

- his brother's words and jealousy
- the king's words and fear
- being conformed to an image that was not his

David passed the test and the distractions that keep many of us from going onto the battlefield. David didn't go and dress up like what he was seeing with his physical eyes. He said "*No, I haven't proved that. When I took out that bear, when I took out that lion, I know how I did it, so that's the way I'm going to go, because that's the image I have. You're not going to change my image. I am going to throw down (fight), but we're going to throw down the way I am used to throwing down. I'm fighting in the way that made me successful.*" This is why <u>what you see</u> is so important. What David saw that would defeat this giant was:

1. his staff
2. five smooth stones
3. a shepherd's bag
4. his sling

Many times what God wants to use as our weapons may look foolish to those who only see with natural eyes. Now, after dealing with his brother's negativity and the king's fear (inner camp enemies) he had to face the enemy outside of the camp.

> **1 Samuel 17:41-44** KJV
>
> *41 And the Philistine came on and drew near unto David; and the man that bare the shield went before him. 42 And when the Philistine looked about, and saw David, he disdained him: for he was but a youth, and ruddy,*

and of a fair countenance. ⁴³ And the Philistine said unto David, Am I a dog, that thou comest to me with staves? And the Philistine cursed David by his gods. ⁴⁴ And the Philistine said to David, Come to me, and I will give thy flesh unto the fowls of the air, and to the beasts of the field.

First of all the enemy (the giant) was offended that David – this little 'pretty boy' was out there ready to fight him. Then he did what Satan tries every time — to intimidate with his words. Intimidation is such a familiar ploy of the enemy. Intimidation is meant to get you to back down and retreat. How many circumstances and situations do you have 'talking back' to you? The enemy knows how powerful words and images are so he tries to paint a picture of gloom and doom for you. He wants you to think that you are like the baby elephant and you can't move; that you are limited, but nothing is further from the truth. **The enemy will speak as long as you stay silent.** So you always have to be aware of this tactic and be ready to fire back at him with your words. You have something to say. You do not have the right to remain silent! Notice what David does...

1 Samuel 17:45-48 ᴷᴶⱽ
⁴⁵ Then said David to the Philistine, Thou comest to me with a sword, and with a spear, and with a shield: but *I*

> *come to thee in the name of the Lord* of hosts, the God of the armies of Israel, whom thou hast defied. ⁴⁶ **This day** will the Lord deliver thee into mine hand; and I will smite thee, and take thine head from thee; and I will give the carcasses of the host of the Philistines this day unto the fowls of the air, and to the wild beasts of the earth; that all the earth may know that there is a God in Israel. ⁴⁷ And all this assembly shall know that the Lord saveth not with sword and spear: for the battle is the Lord's, and he will give you into our hands. ⁴⁸ And it came to pass, when the Philistine arose, and came, and drew nigh to meet David that **David hastened, and ran toward** the army to meet **the Philistine**.

David did not stay silent. He began to tell his giant the picture and the image that he saw in his imagination of what was about to take place. He painted a picture (vision) so clear that his image bothered the enemy so much that the enemy decided to charge at him. David said, with his actions, *bring it on! I've said what I had to say and now it's time to get down to it.* As this giant charged, David didn't even have a second of hesitation. *This is a moment when the two images are going to collide* and David knew that the Lord was on His side. He was able to face danger and not draw back because the image of God was with him, in him, by him and for him! This image was carrying him further than his natural strength could. **There is a place inside you with God where all of the burners are on and there is no turning back because the fuel of the Spirit is carrying you into battle!** This is not a natural battle but one in the Spirit where the God in you does the impossible. There is a supernatural force that propels you forward into battle and collision with the enemy to do him damage and to do damage to the kingdom of darkness.

You have to also have this image/mindset. The mindset where you don't care what it looks like naturally! Where that image of a great big God on the inside of you is bigger than anything that can come against you. That mindset that says you can't be beat, and you can't be defeated. Even if you fall, you're getting back up! You are more than a conqueror, the enemy can't defeat you. The enemy does not know what you are made of (God's image). You may hit the ground, but you are getting back up. You are not staying down, you are getting back up! That's the mindset you possess when you have God's image on the inside of you.

> **1 Samuel 17:49-51** KJV
>
> [49] And David put his hand in his bag, and took thence a stone, and slang it, and smote the Philistine in his forehead, that the stone sunk into his forehead; and he fell upon his face to the earth. [50] So David prevailed

over the Philistine with a sling and with a stone, and smote the Philistine, and slew him; but there was no sword in the hand of David. [51] Therefore David ran, and stood upon the Philistine, and took his sword, and drew it out of the sheath thereof, and slew him, and cut off his head therewith. And when the Philistines saw their champion was dead, they fled.

David reached for his bag which carried his weapon. He grabbed a smooth stone and slung it at the enemy. **There comes a time when you will need to use the weapons that God has given you.** He has given you His word, image, dominion and authority to name a few. You need to know what your weapons are and how and when to use them. In order for David to win this fight he had to see himself winning. Likewise, in order for you to win your battle you will need to see yourself winning. God's sight and your sight need to be the same.

You have to see it
[e] Florence Chadwick was an American long-distance swimmer. She was actually the first woman to swim the English Channel in both directions, setting a record each time. After swimming the English Channel, Florence decided that she was going to go to the coast of California and swim to the Catalina Islands. She set the date for the event. On the day of the event her coach and mom were

there. It was foggy and cold, and the waves were really choppy. She said, "Nonetheless, this is the day that I set. I'm going to do it." So her mom and the coach got in the pace boat and they moved along with her as she started to swim. Florence swam for hours and hours and hours, and then she finally looked at the coach and said, "That's it. I'm done. I can't go any further." The coach said, "Well, are you hurt?" She said, "No." He said, "Well, you don't know this but your stroke is still really strong. I think you can go a little further." So she said, "All right."

Florence swam for hours in the fog, in the cold water, and the choppy waves. Then after a few more hours she stopped and she said, "That is it. I am absolutely exhausted. I can't go any further." After a few encouraging words the coach finally decided to pull her into the boat. As they pulled her into the boat the fog started to lift, and they could see the Catalina Islands ... one mile away. Florence said (probably sadly), **"If I had seen it, I could have made it."**

There are many plans, purposes, and promises that God has for you. They may be currently hidden in what is now a foggy scene and you may not know that you are really close to a breakthrough. *I want to encourage you that you are probably closer than you think.* God has not forgotten you. **Sometimes you have to fight with your eyes closed.** Doing this will limit what you see naturally and the distractions that occur. Trials and tests are designed to weaken your resolve to finish strong. **What you see naturally can encourage you to quit before you get there.** I encourage you again, not to give up the good fight of faith but to hold on to the thoughts, promises and image from God. Know, believe and have faith....*that He who has begun a good work in you will finish what He started. This is the will of God for His Kingdom people.*

Philippians 1:6 ^{KJV}
*Being confident of this very thing, that he which hath begun a **good work** in you will perform it until the day of Jesus Christ:*

May you dominate in life through Christ!

Allen Forbes

www.AFspeaks.com

If you enjoyed reading this book, please leave a favorable review on Amazon.com

Introduction to the King

Maybe by some off chance you picked up this book and you have never met the King. I would like to take this time to introduce you to Him. He came, died and bled for you because He loves you. His name is Jesus and He longs to have a relationship with you. In order to have this relationship with Him you will have to invite Him to come and live in your heart. You can do this by praying and inviting Him in. If you would like to do so, please read the prayer below and then pray it to Him with sincerity.

Prayer
God I am a sinner and I believe that Jesus died for the forgiveness of my sin. I believe that Jesus Christ was raised from the dead and is my Lord and Savior. You loved me so much that you gave your Son so I could be a part of your family. I invite you to come and live in my heart. Please lead and guide me as my new Lord in the kingdom of God.

It is that simple (Romans 10:9). If you prayed and believe this prayer please reach out to us so we can connect with you. In the meantime, find a good bible believing church that you can become a part of.

Welcome to the Kingdom! Enjoy getting to know the King.

Contact us at www.LivingLifeInternational.org

Reference

[a] **The Principles of Self Mastery by Napoleon Hill** page 18 and 20

[b] **Sandbox Personalities by Allen Forbes** Page 33

www.SandboxPersonalities.com

[c] **Law of sympathetic resonance** – Page 43

https://en.wikipedia.org/wiki/Sympathetic_resonance

[d] **Bob Harrison** page 102

http://www.increase.org/

[e] **Florence Chadwick story** Page 121

https://en.wikipedia.org/wiki/Florence_Chadwick

About the Author

Allen Forbes is a Christian author and speaker who is dedicated to encouraging others to recognize and pursue their identity in God. He is a licensed minister, with a background of 20+ years of faithful serving and stewardship in ministry. Allen has spent decades in the business arena in roles that included service, management, sales, and entrepreneurship. He is the co-founder of Living Life International a faith-based nonprofit that inspires, educates and informs. You will find a combination of biblical principles, humor and extensive business wisdom in his books and presentations. Originally from Brooklyn, NY Allen and his family reside in Maryland.

Connect with Allen through social media

https://www.facebook.com/allen.forbes.12

https://twitter.com/AllenForbes

Resources

Free Audio Download

https://sellfy.com/p/648l/

Sandbox Personalities Book

www.sandboxpersonalities.com

www.ingramcontent.com/pod-product-compliance
Lightning Source LLC
LaVergne TN
LVHW051459070426
835507LV00022B/2847